Communist China
in Perspective

COMMUNIST CHINA IN PERSPECTIVE

*The Oreon E. Scott Foundation
Lectures, presented at Washington
University in December, 1961*

by A. Doak Barnett

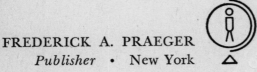

FREDERICK A. PRAEGER
Publisher • New York

BOOKS THAT MATTER

Published in the United States of America in 1962 by
Frederick A. Praeger, Inc., Publisher
64 University Place, New York 3, N.Y.
Second printing, 1963
© 1962 by Frederick A. Praeger, Inc.
All rights reserved
Library of Congress Catalog Card Number: 62-16640

COMMUNIST CHINA IN PERSPECTIVE
is published in two editions:

A Praeger Paperback (PPS-87)
A clothbound edition

This book is Number 110 in the series of
Praeger Publications in Russian History and World Communism

Manufactured in the United States of America

PREFACE

THIS VOLUME is based on three lectures delivered at Washington University, St. Louis, in December, 1961. The lectures were part of the university's annual Oreon E. Scott Foundation Lectures series, open to the public.

The invitation extended to me by Washington University specified, simply, that I discuss China. With misgivings about my qualifications, I decided to attempt a broad analysis of the Chinese revolution, focusing on several basic questions: What is the past out of which Communism emerged in China? What is the nature of the current revolutionary process in that country? And what can one say about the future prospects of the Chinese Communist regime and of China under its rule?

One should not pretend that such questions can really be answered adequately. I decided, however, that there would be value in exploring them. Most of us, specialists and laymen alike, tend to be preoccupied with the latest developments and headlines. It is useful, periodically, to attempt to detach oneself from immediate problems and issues, to try to view the broad sweep of developments in historical perspective.

The response to my three lectures when they were presented at St. Louis was gratifying, and when it was proposed that the lectures be published, I agreed. In preparing this volume, however, I have expanded certain parts of the lectures and revised others. But the essential elements are those which I originally presented at Washington University.

CONTENTS

I

HISTORICAL
PERSPECTIVE

IN VIEWING a tremendous revolutionary upheaval such
as the one now under way in China, it is essential
to place current developments in some sort of historical
perspective. Despite the difficulty of the task, unless one
attempts to relate the forces now at work with past developments and future prospects, there is little basis for
grasping, even partially, the significance of contem-
porary events.

It is clear that Mao Tse-tung and the other leaders
who today control the greatest single concentration of
people on earth are greatly affected by their own particular image of the past out of which they emerged. It
is also apparent that they are moved by a vision of the
future that affects virtually everything they say and do.
Those who would understand the regime these leaders
now control, and the society they are attempting to
create, should also pay close attention to both the past
and the future. Only by doing so is it possible to begin
acquiring some real understanding of the present.

In July, 1949, just before the establishment of a Communist central government in China, Mao declared that
"the gunfire of the October Revolution sent us Marx-

ism-Leninism," and Chinese Communist writers now generally date the beginning of "their" revolution to the period just after the Bolshevik upheaval in Russia. This is certainly understandable. Without doubt, the Russian Revolution did have a significant impact on China. The growth of intense modern nationalism accelerated greatly from about 1919 onward. And the Chinese Communist Party was formally established in 1921.

But, if one attempts to trace the origins of what many Chinese themselves call "The Chinese Revolution"—rather than merely the growth of Marxism-Leninism and an organized Communist movement in China—one must look back more than a century. What can legitimately be called the Chinese revolution had been under way for more than a hundred years before the Chinese Communists were able to seize control of it and come to power. One might say, in fact, that it was the gunfire of the small British naval vessels that fought the Opium War in the early 1840's, forcing China to open its doors to Western penetration, that marked the real beginning of the Chinese revolution.

At times, the stream of history seems very similar to what some writers like to call the "stream of consciousness": It is confused and confusing, often unintelligible, fed by innumerable tributary streams of influence that are frequently hard to identify, and yet it does possess a logic of its own, and its main course can be defined and analyzed. The essential story of the Chinese revolution during the past century or more can be examined in terms of two closely interrelated, interacting factors—the breakdown of the old order in China caused by the impact of the Western world superimposed upon a serious domestic crisis, and the agonizing struggle of the Chinese people to come to terms with the technological and economic superiority and the philosophical and ideological challenge that they discovered in the West once their own isolation had been shattered.

In the mid-nineteenth century, a process of slow but basic political, economic, and social change was set in motion in China. This process stimulated and released innumerable new forces and ideas, and it began inexorably to undermine traditional Chinese society. Slowly, the Chinese revolution gained momentum, and finally, in the late nineteenth and early twentieth centuries, it took effective political shape. This was long before the Chinese Communist Party was founded and, in fact, long before the 1917 Revolution had taken place in Russia.

In the Chinese revolution, the Communists were actually latecomers on the scene, and for quite a while they were relatively unimportant. It was certainly not inevitable from the start that the Chinese revolution would become Communist-led and Communist-controlled—as it has, in fact, during the past two decades. The Communists ultimately succeeded for a variety of reasons: the repeated and serious failures of other leaders and movements to cope with China's ever-growing problems; the historical accident that the Sino-Japanese War in the 1930's and 1940's, along with the breakdown of the old order in China, created conditions that were ripe for exploitation by a highly organized revolutionary movement such as the one the Communists were able to create; and the fact that the Chinese Communist Party itself, after early failures, evolved an extremely effective organizational apparatus and a revolutionary strategy skillfully adapted to the existing situation and forces at work in China.

Perhaps the dimensions of the changes in Chinese society during the past century can be grasped more readily if one recognizes that not one, but several revolutions—to use the term in its broadest sense, meaning revolutionary changes in society, not simply political movements—have been going on simultaneously since the 1840's. In this period of a little over a hundred years—very brief in historical terms—not only has the oldest and probably the most stable social and political system in history been destroyed, but China has been attempting to cope with a variety of radical social changes that were spread over several centuries in the West. If one can take the liberty of making very crude analogies with Europe, it is not too far-fetched to say that a renaissance, a reformation, a commercial and industrial revolution, a democratic-liberal political revolution, and a scientific revolution—to say nothing of the Communist revolution—have all, in a sense, been developing more or less simultaneously within China during the past century. Since the 1840's, the Chinese revolution, in other words, has been ideological, cultural, social, and economic—as well as political.

The causes, both internal and external, of the disintegration of the old order and the emergence of the new in China have been extremely numerous and complex. It is not possible here to do more than touch upon just a few aspects of the story. But perhaps even a brief review of a few of its highlights may illuminate some of the basic forces that not only helped to shape the

Chinese revolution before the Communists came to power, but inevitably are still influencing the course of revolution in China today. It is important that we understand these forces. If the West is to be successful in its attempts to influence significantly the outcome of the virtually world-wide revolution that is now under way in the non-Western areas of the world, it is essential to learn the lessons that emerge from the story of the past century of revolution in China.

Although it is normal procedure to reserve one's conclusions until the last, it is difficult to do more than present conclusions when space is limited. Perhaps it is justifiable, therefore, before even attempting to present a sketchy outline of the major bench marks in the Chinese revolution since the 1840's, to summarize a few of the major lessons that stand out as one examines and ponders the course of events in China over the past century.

First of all, the Chinese revolution dramatically highlights the fact that the West's values, institutions, and material culture are powerful forces indeed in the world we live in; moreover, although we do not always recognize it, they exert a strongly subversive influence in the tradition-oriented, economically underdeveloped, premodern areas of the world. The values embodied in Western nationalism, liberalism, democracy, religion, economic thought, and science have proved repeatedly, in many other areas besides China, to be highly dynamic; they tend, almost inevitably, to subvert the relatively static values and goals underlying most tradition-rooted non-Western societies, whether these societies are comparatively primitive ones, such as those in the newly

emerging countries of Africa, or highly developed societies, such as the one that existed in premodern China.

Not only do "ideas have legs" (as one writer put it),
but our material culture has them, too, and by itself is
a surprisingly effective carrier of ideas—a fact that is
not always adequately appreciated. Simple exposure to
Western machines and gadgets is a major cause of one
of the strongest forces released in non-Western societies
by the impact of the West: the revolution of rising expectations.

Another of these forces, and one of the most con-
tagious of all Western exports, is the idea of nationalism.
Without trying to be Biblical, one might say that the
experience in China, as well as elsewhere, proves con-
vincingly that nationalism begets nationalism, coloni-
alism begets anticolonialism, and imperialism begets
anti-imperialism. And, once produced by the impact of
the West, nationalism, anticolonialism, and anti-imperialism are among the most potent forces with which
the West must then deal.

The experience in China also indicates that the
process of revolution created by the West's impact upon
premodern societies is frequently deceptive and is widely
misunderstood by the actual carriers of the virus of
change. Initially, the most dramatic visible trend in
many countries that come into contact with the West
for the first time is simply the disintegration of the old
society; there is little surface evidence of the strong
new forces developing. But it is during such periods
of disintegration, and apparent weakness, that a slow
process of ideological, economic, and social revolution
takes place. New classes and leadership groups emerge

—classes and groups destined ultimately to become the key instruments of change, to take the lead in crystallizing the forces of change into revolutionary political movements.

The principal centers of ferment and the headquarters of revolution in this process, judging by the Chinese experience, are usually the new modernized, or semimodernized, cities that inevitably emerge in premodern societies under the impact of the West. And within such cities it is the Western-influenced universities and other educational institutions that generally produce the beginnings of a new leadership elite that is fervently dedicated to change and rejects much of its nation's past.

The Chinese experience also indicates that in large agrarian societies where serious crises develop in the rural sector of society, and where a spirit of revolt grows among the peasantry, the peasants may also become a potentially strong revolutionary force—one that can be aroused, organized, and exploited by shrewd and skillful revolutionary leaders to form the mass basis for a radical political movement.

If the Chinese experience can be generalized at all, another lesson is that while, politically, Western democratic ideals, institutions, and practices exercise a potent attraction to the newly emerging elites in revolutionary societies and are often highly effective in subverting traditional authoritarian political systems, at the same time, they are exceptionally difficult to integrate into societies that lack certain basic prerequisites for political democracy and are undergoing the difficult transition from traditionalism to modernism.

There is a great danger that the revolutionary forces unleashed by the impact of Western democratic values may, as in China, produce failure and disillusion rather than success and fulfillment. Also, in the vacuum created by the destruction of the traditional political system and the failure of democratic experiments, revolutionaries may turn toward modern forms of authoritarianism, militarism, or totalitarianism to achieve their goals. Today, in almost every revolutionary situation in the world, Communism stands in the wings ready to step in, to capitalize on the failure of democratic experiments and exploit the frustrations caused by unfulfilled revolutionary hopes motivated by nationalism and the desire for modernization and reform.

A final important lesson emerges from this review of the Chinese experience. War, without doubt, is one of the greatest immediate causes of modern political revolutions—and, most specifically, Communist-led revolutions—both because it often creates a dramatic crisis in the old order and because the destruction, inflation, and disintegration it generally produces provide unparalled opportunities for determined revolutionary leaders to exploit.

With these major points in mind, let us examine specifically the revolutionary process in China as it has unfolded over the past century.

Before the nineteenth-century impact of the West, the old order in China was a remarkably stable one. The idea that it remained completely static over the centuries is certainly not supported by the available evidence, but there is general agreement that for roughly 2,000 years prior to the modern period certain essential features of China's political system, social structure, and economy were, in fact, remarkably unchanging. There were numerous domestic upheavals, and rulers came and went in a process of political change that has been labeled the "dynastic cycle," but such change was generally superficial. The force of tradition was so great that new rulers, instead of trying to alter the basic character of Chinese society, almost inevitably accepted it and merely tried to restore the grandeur of the past.

The political structure in traditional China was highly centralized and authoritarian. At the top was the imperial monarchy, ruled by one man whose power, in theory at least, was limited only by the so-called "mandate of heaven." Actual rule of the empire was largely in the hands of the relatively small educated elite that made up the official bureaucracy. Recruited by a unique and remarkable examination system, this elite was thoroughly indoctrinated in the official state ideology, Confucianism, and was highly conservative.

However, despite the extreme centralization of political power and the lack of democratic mass participation in government, the actual functions of government were generally limited. In theory, the bureaucracy was responsible for a very complex system of political supervision and thought control designed to affect the entire population. But in practice, especially when the central government was weak, the bureaucracy's main functions were simply to collect taxes, to supervise the construction of certain basic public works (especially irrigation works), and to insure the maintenance of fundamental law and order. At the bottom level of government, below the *hsien,* or district offices, the management of public affairs was frequently left in the hands of conservative local societies and organizations.

Under this traditional authoritarian system, there was no accepted process for peaceful, orderly change of government or political power. There was, however, a long history of peasant rebellion when conditions became intolerable, of underground, secret-society opposition to unjust political authority, and of change of government by revolt when the existing top leadership became ineffectual and weak. Rarely, however, did even the overthrow of dynasties cause basic social change in China. New rulers almost inevitably attempted to restore the *status quo ante*.

The two key elements in the traditional social structure in China were: the educated scholar-gentry, a very large number of them landowners, who not only provided the reservoir for recruits to the ruling government bureaucracy but also usually dominated local affairs; and the huge mass of peasants, generally poor and illiterate, who, in addition to struggling to make ends meet for themselves, provided the economic surplus upon which the state existed.

Economically, traditional China was overwhelmingly agricultural, and the prevailing pattern of agricultural enterprise was one characterized by private ownership of land and small-scale farming. It was a technologically backward economy, plagued by a recurring problem of farm tenancy and concentration of land ownership. As population increased rapidly during the eighteenth and nineteenth centuries, the shortage of land became increasingly serious.

During the nineteenth century, this tradition-rooted

society began to experience an internal political crisis, a period of dynastic decline comparable to many that had taken place in China during the past. The Manchu government, which had been in power for roughly two centuries, became increasingly ineffectual, inefficient, and corrupt. Peasant unrest and rebellion of a traditional sort spread rapidly, stimulated by increasing overpopulation and land concentration, as well as endemic poverty and the deterioration of the government.

This was the situation when, in the 1840's, a few small gunboats from the West forcibly destroyed China's self-imposed isolation. Theoretically, if China had been able to continue its existence in "splendid isolation," it might have undergone a traditional "time of troubles" and emerged, ultimately, with a new dynasty but with its old society intact. With the benefit of historical hindsight, however, one can say rather confidently that this was no more than a theoretical possibility in the nineteenth century. By that time, the dynamics of the economic, technological, and ideological revolutions generated in Europe had already begun to spread in all directions, and it was only a matter of time before their impact would reach China.

In the century following 1840, the agents of revolutionary Western influence in China were marvelously diverse. They included not only Western troops and diplomats but businessmen, missionaries, teachers, doctors, and other elements that are generally viewed in the West as conservative supporters of stability and order. In China, they all (most of them unwittingly) served as instruments of revolutionary change in either a negative or positive sense—contributing to the breakdown of the old order, serving as channels for the introduction of new ideas, values, goals, and institutions, and helping to stimulate the growth of new social groups and the initiation of significant processes of social change.

Successive military and political defeats by foreign powers after 1840 created a crisis of confidence in China's leadership. They also highlighted China's technological backwardness and military impotence in the face of the West. The creation of foreign concessions and "treaty ports" did more than shake Chinese confidence in the government—it formed the basis for a systematic, legalized Western political penetration and interference in China. Old Confucian concepts and values that had hardly been questioned for centuries began to be discredited because they were clearly incapable of coping effectively with the modern outside world.

Economically, the opening of China to foreign trade on an unprecedented scale led to the importation of a wide range of new, manufactured products, and with these came new ideas and institutions. In addition, cheap goods from the West helped to undermine China's old handicraft industries and disrupt the traditional economy. Modern transport and industry slowly began to appear. New cities grew, and new classes developed in them.

Cities in the process of becoming modernized, especially "treaty ports" such as Shanghai and Tientsin, were the first real centers of the slow, almost imperceptible revolutionary ferment that began to take place in China, socially and economically as well as politically.

In these cities, a so-called "comprador" class of merchant middlemen, who served as a link between foreign businessmen and the Chinese hinterland, first sprang up; later, the beginnings of a modern Chinese business class, an urban proletariat, and even a small urban middle class appeared. These new classes were not large, but they were important instruments and symbols of change.

Perhaps most important of all was the growth of a Western-educated elite in China. The members of this new group became the main carriers of revolutionary ideas and ideals. Especially after the turn of the twentieth century, thousands of young Chinese went abroad to Japan, Europe, the United States, and ultimately the Soviet Union. Thousands more were educated in new, Western-type schools established in China by missionaries. Even the government itself finally decided to abandon traditional Confucian concepts of education and began to support the development of a state educational system patterned on Western models. Most of the products of this new Western education—whether obtained in China, Japan, or the West—were strongly antitraditionalist and fervently in favor of modernization and change. They formed a new Chinese intelligentsia, very different indeed from the old Chinese elite composed of tradition-oriented, Confucianist scholar-bureaucrats.

Of special importance in China was the national student movement, which grew in strength from 1919 onward and played an extremely important role in both stirring up political ferment and providing new leadership. Also out of China's new Westernized universities

came the so-called "Chinese renaissance," which began
with a movement to popularize the written vernacular
language, and then became the main force pressing for
the acceptance of Western ideas and values under the
slogan of "science and democracy." Ultimately, these
universities became the principal centers for the introduction of theoretical Marxism and Communism into
China.

It was among the new urban groups, and particularly
among the members of the modern intelligentsia, that
powerful new ideological forces developed. The idea of
nationalism was one of the foremost of these. Tradi-
tionally, it is true, China had had a strong sense of
cultural unity and superiority, but the modern concept
of nationalism was an import that came from the West
and was soon turned against it. After the Chinese had
been subjected to one humiliation after another by
both the Western powers and Japan, the idea of building
China into a strong nation-state that could modernize,
acquire military strength, and develop economically,
and thus be able to stand up against the predatory influences of outside powers, became one of the strongest
motivating forces among the modern Chinese intellectual class. From them, it spread to others. A demand for
political, economic, and social reform also became increasingly insistent. The members of China's emerging
new modern elite were almost universally agreed on a
number of goals: the development of science, modern
technology, and national power; the introduction of
constitutional government with democratic mass participation in politics; industrialization and economic

growth; and agrarian reform that would provide land to the tiller.

The political revolution in China was a direct outgrowth and reflection of these many ideological, social, and economic forces—forces that were produced by the simultaneous dynastic decline of the old regime and the powerful impact of the West. It is obviously not possible to trace, in even the barest detail here, the course of this revolution since the mid-nineteenth century. However, at least a few of the most notable milestones should be mentioned.

The first was the Taiping Rebellion, an enormous peasant upheaval that lasted over a decade during the 1850's and 1860's. Led by a frustrated, old-time Chinese scholar who adopted a pseudo-Christian ideology and promoted his own form of primitive communism, the Taiping Rebellion was essentially a traditional peasant uprising, comparable in some respects to many that had taken place in past periods of dynastic decline. If it had succeeded in overthrowing the Manchu Dynasty—and it came very close to doing so—it is not certain whether the immediate result would have been a basic change in Chinese society or merely the inauguration of a new dynastic regime. Ultimately, in any case, it failed. But there is no doubt that it did hasten the undermining of the Manchus' power. It also stimulated the development of new local leaders and regional armed forces, which sprang up to meet the Taiping threat and then, in turn, created new pressures upon the Imperial Government for change and reform.

In the 1890's, an abortive attempt was finally made to reform the Chinese Government from the top, to

modernize the administration, and to introduce con-
stitutionalism. Under the influence of a small group of
intellectual leaders, most of whom still hoped that China
could introduce selected modern institutions and techniques and yet still preserve traditional Confucian
values, the Emperor issued a remarkable series of reform edicts. But the conservative, reactionary elements,
who opposed all significant change, strongly reasserted
themselves, and he was quickly deposed by the Empress
Dowager.

However, another political movement, with much
more fundamental goals, was also taking shape in the
1890's, and it gained strength steadily during the first
decade of the twentieth century. Under Sun Yat-sen,
and other leaders who had been educated for the most
part either in the West or in Japan, this group called
for not only the overthrow of the Manchu Dynasty, but
also a fundamental reform of Chinese society. Ultimately, it was to grow into the Kuomintang, or Chinese
Nationalist Party, which was to become the dominant
force in modern Chinese politics until the Communist
take-over in 1949.

Sun formulated a program that was summarized in
three major slogans, embodying ideas that even by the
first decades of this century had acquired real potency
in China: "nationalism," "democracy," and "people's
livelihood." He called for mass participation in political
life, the modernization and industrialization of China,
agrarian reform, and the reassertion of China's inde-
pendence and self-respect in international affairs. Although led by members of the emerging new Chinese
intellectual elite, Sun's movement allied itself with

many diverse forces for change in China. These included some of the traditional secret societies, which had a strong xenophobic dislike not only of Westerners but also of the Manchus, who, while they had ruled China for close to three centuries, were still considered foreigners. Finally, in 1911, Sun's movement was successful—or so it seemed at the time. The Manchu Dynasty was overthrown and replaced by a republic.

Perhaps it would be more correct to say, however, that the old regime in China simply disintegrated from the combined erosive effects of internal decay and external pressures. Sun and his followers merely gave the final push that toppled it. They certainly did not have a revolutionary movement strongly enough organized at the time of the final collapse to create the kind of new order that was their goal. The events that immediately followed the Manchu downfall soon made this evident.

China's urgent need, after the disintegration of the old dynasty in 1911, was for a rapid national reintegration, and Sun Yat-sen, together with the other revolutionary political leaders who emerged from this period as national heroes, called bravely for new political institutions, new leadership, and new policies of orderly, directed social and economic change. But it quickly became clear that they lacked the plans, organizational strength, or political and military support necessary to achieve their aims. Instead of being reintegrated, China entered a long and disillusioning period of near chaos. The central government became a mere shadow government, while real power passed into the hands of local warlords, who created personal armies and established regional regimes that assumed control over large portions of the country.

The immediate result, therefore, was not the solution of China's growing problem but an intensification of them. The forward-looking intellectuals who had had such high hopes for rapid modernization, reform, and development were bitterly disappointed by this initial failure of parliamentary government, and as a consequence they became increasingly tempted to turn toward radicalism in their search for solutions to China's problems. China's peasants, who for decades had been suffering the consequences of China's agricultural crisis, experienced new forms of oppression under warlordism, so that they, too, became increasingly restive and ripe for revolutionary exploitation.

The Western democratic powers appeared entirely unwilling or unable, during this period, to help the new Western-oriented leaders in China achieve their goals. To a large number of China's emerging leaders, in fact, most of the Western nations and Japan seemed to be preoccupied solely with a desire to exploit China's weakness to their own advantage.

This was the situation in China when the "ten days that shook the world" took place in Russia. The Bolshevik Revolution of 1917 had an immediate and sizable influence on the Chinese, but its impact was by no means confined, in this period, simply to the small Chinese Communist Party, formed in 1921 with Comintern help. Ironically, perhaps its greatest influence during these early years was exerted through the Kuomintang.

Disillusioned with Western parliamentary methods,

the Nationalist leaders, as well as the Communists, discovered in the Soviet Union a new model for political action. They received direct support and encouragement from Moscow. With the Comintern acting as midwife, a short-lived political alliance took place in 1923 between the Nationalist Party, which then clearly represented the main force of political revolution in China, and the small, newly formed Communist Party. Even more important, the Nationalist Party itself was reorganized in 1924, with the help of Russian advisers, into a mass political organization that borrowed heavily from the Soviet model.

The introduction of modern concepts and techniques of mass political action ushered in a quite new period in the Chinese revolution. The Kuomintang, helped by the Communists until their split during early 1927, organized a political movement that was stronger and more effective than any in China's previous history. It defeated the warlord-dominated central government, took the first necessary steps toward the reunification of the country, established a modernized government, and started to develop modern communications and industry. It introduced Sun's Three People's Principles as the new state-supported ideology and began to restore China's rights and dignity in its relations with the foreign powers. During the decade between 1927 and 1937, in fact, the Nationalist government made notable progress in many areas, and it unquestionably became the primary focus of hope for the large majority of China's educated elite and new urban classes, which demanded reform, development, and modernization.

Then came the Sino-Japanese War in 1937 and, with

it, invasion, destruction, and general disruption. What had started out with great enthusiasm and hope soon turned into a story of failure, disillusion, and disintegration once again. By the end of the war, eight years later, the Nationalist Government in China was in a shambles. While ostensibly one of the war's victors, it was, in fact, on the verge of defeat.

✓ The effects of the war on China were devastating. The general economic situation deteriorated badly. China's agrarian crisis became increasingly serious. Rampant inflation created acute economic insecurity, with effects that were particularly disastrous to some of the groups that had been among the Nationalists' strong supporters at the start. Forced back into China's hinterland, the Nationalists became increasingly dependent on agricultural taxation and on the support of conservative landlords to levy it; consequently, the idea of implementing land reform, originally inspired by Sun Yat-sen himself, was indefinitely postponed. Within both the Nationalist Party and the government, there was a slow but steady erosion of morale and efficiency. In wide areas of China, local leaders once again reasserted their power and strengthened local regimes based on personal armies. The intellectuals of China became steadily more disillusioned and bitter. And to cope with this deteriorating situation, the Nationalists resorted to increasingly oppressive methods, which resulted in the alienation of one group after another but failed to bring the situation under control.

By the end of the war, the Nationalists' failures loomed much larger in the minds of most Chinese than their accomplishments. They had failed to unify the country or, in fact, to develop genuine unity even within the Nationalist Party itself. They had failed to develop their rudimentary ideology into an effective program of national reform, and Sun's Three People's Principles became increasingly empty slogans to which few responded. They had failed to develop an efficient party and government administrative apparatus that could effectively reach rural as well as urban areas in China—at least those remaining under their control. They had failed to carry out the kind of land program that might have helped alleviate China's basic agrarian problems. And they had failed to retain the support of the new, modernized intellectual elite in China.

There is no doubt that much of the blame for these failures can be attributed directly to the effects of the war itself. But this fact did not change the situation that actually existed in China by 1945, nor did it moderate the disillusionment of the Chinese people. What had started out less than twenty years before, in 1927, as a new order holding out hope for a brave new world was by 1945 already another old regime tottering on the verge of collapse.

All of this is essential background to an understanding of the reasons for Communist success in China. It was during the Sino-Japanese War and immediately thereafter—when Chinese nationalism was raised to a high pitch, the Kuomintang was disintegrating, and popular disillusion was growing—that the Chinese Communists pursued the program, built the Party organization, and acquired the military strength that enabled them ultimately (in the period 1946–49) to embark upon a direct test of strength with the Nationalist regime, a test from which they emerged victorious and established the new Communist regime.

The strategy evolved by Mao Tse-tung and the other top Chinese Communist leaders during this period was consciously shaped to fit the specific situation existing in China, to capitalize on the failures of the Nationalists, and to exploit some of the basic revolutionary forces that had been building up in China for decades.

During the first years of their existence in the 1920's, the Communists in China, under the direct and close tutelage of the Comintern, failed repeatedly in their efforts to gain power through a strategy based primarily on the idea of building a party of the proletariat and organizing urban insurrection. In the late 1920's and early 1930's, however, they were forced by their own failures into the Chinese countryside, and there they evolved a new strategy emphasizing several key elements: appeals to Chinese patriotism and to China's new nationalistic, reform-minded intellectuals; a land reform program to exploit the latent forces of unrest and revolt among China's peasantry; the development of a strong peasant-based revolutionary army; the establishment of definite revolutionary bases—so-called "liberated areas"—in the countryside; and the employment of flexible tactics of armed struggle based on shrewd concepts of protracted guerrilla warfare.

The Sino-Japanese War provided the Chinese Communists with their great opportunity, and they took full advantage of it. At the beginning of the war, the Communist Party in China had consisted of a mere 40,000 or so members, isolated in a remote and poverty-stricken area of northwest China; by 1945, its membership had grown to well over a million members. It had built a powerful guerrilla army. It controlled major portions of the rural hinterland in north China. And it had convinced a significant number of China's young intellectuals that Communism represented the wave of the future, that it was a movement able to achieve some of China's basic new goals: national power and self-respect, social reform, and economic development.

It is instructive to recall the major slogans used by the Chinese Communists to propagate their program during this period (the period before they actually achieved power): "new democracy," "anti-imperialism," "antifeudalism," and "antibureaucratic capitalism." These slogans were designed to appeal to widespread and powerful new drives that had steadily gained strength during the past century of revolution in China. They were consciously aimed at exploiting the frustration of millions of Chinese who had acquired new goals and aspirations but were disillusioned by the repeated failures of past efforts to achieve them.

Prior to 1949, the Chinese Communist Party carefully soft-pedaled, outside its own ranks, many of its basic Marxist-Leninist, Communist aims. It was only after the Party had gained power, and was able to establish an apparatus of totalitarian organization and control, that such basic aims as collectivization, socialization, and political dictatorship came to the fore.

In summary, if one looks at the century-old modern Chinese revolution in historical perspective, it is eminently clear that the forces of revolutionary change the Communists were able to expoit to gain power predated the establishment of the Chinese Communist Party by many decades. The destruction of the old order, caused essentially by the impact of the West—although helped along by internal decay as well—created many new factors and pressures for change in Chinese society: new intellectual and economic classes that demanded basic reform; strong nationalism; a slow but steady trend toward increased involvement of the masses in national life; rising expectations for economic development and betterment, especially among China's new urban classes; and new democratic social and political values. There was a serious gap, however, between the new aspirations and the actual achievements, and growing frustration arose from the disillusioning realization that the achievement of China's new goals would be a long and difficult task.

It was the repeated failures of other revolutionary groups to cope successfully with China's pressing problems that provided the Communists with their opportunity to make a successful bid for power. And in this process, the Sino-Japanese War played a crucial role. Without any doubt, Communism thrives best in the social chaos created by war. It is certainly no accident that almost all the important existing Communist regimes, including those in the Soviet Union, China, and Eastern Europe, were established in the wake of devastating warfare.

Another conclusion—or perhaps I should say another question—emerges from this review of the Chinese revolution, and it is one to give us pause. We in the West talk a great deal, and rightly so, about the world Communist revolution. However, we are hardly aware of, and only partially understand, what might be called the world democratic revolution that we ourselves have been, and still are, creating.

In a sense, this is not surprising. Our revolutionary impact upon the world has been, to a very large extent, unplanned, undirected, and even unconscious. But it is essential that we recognize that not only our government representatives, and armed forces, but also our businessmen, missionaries, educators, and all other elements of our society that come into contact with the non-Western world are actually powerful agents and instruments of revolutionary change. Almost everywhere in the non-Western world, including China, we have unwittingly helped to break down the fabric of traditional societies and to set in motion strong forces of change.

But there still remains a question, I fear—and a question of vital importance to the future—as to whether the revolutionary impact of the West on the non-Western world will prove in the long run to be more destructive than constructive; whether, in brief, it will be more successful in breaking down the structures of old societies than in assisting in the creation of new ones.

There is little doubt that throughout the non-Western world we are contributing to the growth of intense nationalism, new democratic goals, and rising economic aspirations. But are we doing all that we can or should to help the leaders of new nations create the social, economic, and political institutions that are required to achieve these new goals and aspirations? In many respects, the democratic world revolution could prove to be a very dangerous thing. The essential danger lies in the fact that if the old order is destroyed more rapidly than the new can be constructed, modern totalitarian forces—Communism, in particular—may move in to do the job. The Communists are particularly adroit at exploiting the failures of existing regimes in almost every conceivable sort of revolutionary situation. They are always ready to promise that the millennium can be achieved if only totalitarian political methods are adopted. And they are all too often poised ready to capture control of revolutionary forces that are stimulated by the West, but are frequently not sufficiently backed or aided by the non-Communist nations.

This, in effect, is what happened in China. For over a century, the prime external influences that provided the driving force behind the Chinese revolution emanated from the non-Communist West. Since 1949, however, the Chinese revolution, under Communist control, has been merged with the world Communist revolution, and because of the power and dynamism of the new Chinese Communist regime, China now seems likely to remain under Communist rule for a long time to come.

II

CONTINUITY AND CHANGE

THE CHINESE Communists have been in power only a little over a decade, but they have already made an indelible imprint on Chinese society. In this brief period, China has undergone a more far-reaching, rapid, and thorough process of change than at any time in its long history. Every aspect of Chinese society has been affected, and virtually every one of China's 650–700 million people has been touched in significant ways.

There are few instances in history, in fact, where the process of social, political, and economic change has appeared to be so drastic, rapid, and extensive. The Chinese Communist aim has been to alter, fundamentally, the entire nature of Chinese society: its political system—the exercise of leadership and the distribution of power; its economic structure—the ownership, organization, and management of production, as well as the distribution of output; its social structure—the pattern of existing classes and groups and their interrelationships; and its basic ideology and system of values —the common assumptions generally held about the nature of man and his relationship to the universe, to society, and to his fellow man.

It is clear that to the Chinese themselves, one of the regime's most important accomplishments has simply been the restoration of centralized rule over most of the traditional Chinese empire—that is, the reunification of the country. With the exception of Outer Mongolia and Formosa, virtually all the areas the Chinese for centuries have considered to be a part of China, including some clearly colonial regions such as Tibet, have once again been brought under effective central rule. The reunification process has involved the destruction of all the local warlord governments and regional regimes that have plagued China in recent decades, as in past periods of dynastic decline when the central government has been weak.

The political, social, and economic leadership of China has changed hands at almost every level, from top to bottom, during these past thirteen years. Those who held the reins of power at the central, provincial, and local levels before 1949 have been displaced, and an almost entirely new leadership group—the Chinese Communist Party and its various supporters—has assumed control. In short, a new political elite, a new ruling "class," has taken over.

The regime that the Chinese Communists have established is the first effective totalitarian regime, at least in the modern sense, in Chinese history. While the Chinese Nationalists, who preceded the Communists, borrowed from the Russian political model and attempted to build a mass party based on so-called "democratic centralism," they never, in fact, established a genuinely totalitarian apparatus. This was partly because they were ambivalent about their aims—being under pressure to be both democratic in the Western sense and centralist in the Soviet sense, with the result that they were actually neither—and partly because they were not notably successful in their attempts to apply mass totalitarian organizational techniques to China.

The Chinese Communists, however, have had no such ambivalence, and they have been almost frighteningly successful in their organizational efforts. They have built a huge and efficient Leninist mass party that now contains more than 17 million highly disciplined and tightly controlled members directed by a handful of all-powerful Party leaders in the Politburo and the Central Committee at the top. Factionalism and clique rivalries, which appeared to be endemic in China prior to 1949, have been kept under strict control. And a type of Party discipline that most observers, before the Communist take-over, would have labeled "un-Chinese" has been successfully instituted.

The entire government structure in China has been reorganized on the Soviet model, but with significant Chinese variations. During the first years of Chinese Communist rule, it actually appeared as though Peking's rulers were determined to create a virtual carbon copy of the executive, administrative, legal, and other political institutions and processes developed in Stalinist Russia. It has since become clear that many of these new institutions and processes are destined to undergo significant permutations in the Chinese environment. But the influence of the Soviet model remains strong, and the new institutions in China, based on that model, represent a great innovation in governmental organization for China. These institutions have expanded the

functions of government enormously—more than most
people would have thought possible a few years ago.
✓ An even more striking innovation has been the creation of innumerable mass political organizations, under
the Chinese Communist Party's control, encompassing
virtually every identifiable group in the country. These
serve as unprecedented channels for extending the outreach of central political power down to the level of
the villages and to the huge mass of individuals who
make up the world's most populous nation. At the same
time, remarkable new techniques and methods for
propagandizing and indoctrinating the population have
been developed to a level of great effectiveness.

Since 1949, also, the strongest and most unified, centralized, modernized, and politicized army in Chinese
history has been created by the Communists out of the
original guerrilla units they utilized in their struggle
for power. The transition from revolutionary guerrilla
forces to a modernized national defense force has been
very rapid, and the creation of a new type of national
army in Communist China has had a great impact
within the country as well as upon China's role in world
affairs.

As future historians look back on this period, however, many of these general political developments—
these large institutional changes—may prove to be no
more important, and perhaps less profound in their
effects upon Chinese society, than many other results
of the current political revolution. Particularly note-
worthy among these other results have been the accelerated rate of politicization, bureaucratization, and regimentation of the masses and of almost every aspect of

life in China; the great increase in involvement in national as well as local political and economic affairs of ordinary peasants and workers; and the creation of an unprecedented level of national political consciousness among what the Chinese call the *lao pai hsing* (the "old hundred names"), the common people. The Communists in China are true believers in, and practitioners of, "totalism," involving maximum control and supervision of ordinary people's lives, maximum involvement of the entire Chinese population in state-directed activities, maximum control over people's thoughts and behavior, and maximum mobilization of China's millions to serve the purposes of the nation's new Communist regime.

The changes in the Chinese economy during these past thirteen years have been no less drastic and far-reaching than those in political life. The entire economy has been restructured. Here again, the Soviet system has provided the primary model, but there have been many important adaptations to the Chinese situation. Socialization and industrialization have been pushed with great speed and energy. State ownership of the means of production has replaced private enterprise in every important sector of the economy. National planning has been instituted and applied to every aspect of national development, and, while far from being perfected, it has already resulted in an unprecedented degree of state mobilization, allocation, and direction of China's material and human resources. Property and income have been drastically redistributed, and, one might add, wealth has been dramatically leveled.

The structure of economic institutions and the organization and management of almost all economic activities have been fundamentally altered. The socialization of industry and the collectivization and communization of agriculture have changed the daily life of the great majority of individuals in China's huge working population in a most basic way. Industrialization, together with the development of modern transportation and communications, has proceeded at an impressive speed, spreading modern technology and mechanization from the relatively few and isolated areas where modernization had taken root prior to 1949 to the many new centers scattered throughout China's tremendous interior. Science and technology have been almost deified, and they are being energetically promoted with all the resources the regime can muster.

These and many other basic political and economic changes have been accompanied by fundamental changes in China's social system. A new class structure has already emerged. Some traditional class groups have, for all practical purposes, disappeared, while the role of others in Chinese society has been basically changed. The traditional landlord-gentry class that dominated much of rural China in the past has been, to use the Communists' own terminology, "eliminated as a class." In its place, an entirely new leadership group, composed of Party members, cadres, and activists recruited to a considerable extent from China's poor peasants and youth, has become the repository of social and economic, as well as political, power and influence in rural China.

The business, industrial, and commercial classes—not only the small modern business groups, which only recently began to emerge, but also China's traditional old-fashioned merchants and economic entrepreneurs—have been absorbed almost in their entirety into the new economic bureaucracy of the state. China's pre-Communist intellectuals, a great number of whom were educated in Western ideas and ideals (all of which the Communists now vehemently condemn), have been extensively utilized by the new regime, but they have also been subjected to vigorous reindoctrination and severe political controls. A new young Communist intelligentsia, produced by China's expanded and reorganized educational system—a system that stresses a combination of political indoctrination and technical training—has slowly begun to replace them.

The new ruling elite of the country, recruited during the almost continuous class struggles engineered by the Communists ever since they started their revolution, consists of perhaps 5 per cent of the population—the Communist Party and its closest supporters—but it completely dominates the government, the army, the mass organizations, and all the other new political, economic, and social institutions established by the Communists in China. This is certainly not a classless society. There appears to be little prospect, in fact, of it ever becoming one. But it is a society whose class structure is very different from any in China's past. There is a cult of proletarianism and considerable social mobility, but advancement and success are based solely upon criteria set by the Communists: ideological reliability and political or technical performance, as judged by the rulers of the new regime.

Almost all the traditional, nongovernmental social institutions that were so important in China in the past have gone into eclipse. Guilds and secret societies, as well as clan, religious, and regional associations, and the new institutions that developed on Western models in the period prior to 1949 either have been destroyed and replaced by the new mass political organizations established by the Communists or have been reorganized, brought under strict control, and in effect absorbed into the new mass organization system that has penetrated virtually every area—geographical or social —of China.

The family, the bedrock of traditional Chinese society for centuries, is currently undergoing a fundamental transformation. The Communists, being realists, are not trying to eliminate the family; they still recognize that there are certain essential roles that only the family can play, even in a society such as the one they are trying to create. But they *are* consciously attempting to change the character of the family in China. Most specifically, they are trying as rapidly as possible to minimize the family's functions and to make it clearly subordinate to other political and economic institutions. They are also attempting, obviously with some success, to create a new generation whose loyalties to the Party and the state will be so strong as to take precedence automatically over loyalties to the family or any other group.

These are a few of the most dramatic social changes now taking place at an accelerating pace in China. There are many others, however, that may seem to be of lesser importance at the moment, but may be of very great significance indeed in the long run. For example, an

entirely new role is being created in China for women—
for half the population, in short. Women are being
pushed out of the home and into public life—into political, economic, and social activities of all sorts. The
traditional relationship of different age groups also
appears to be changing basically. The crucial roles in
public affairs are now played by the youth, whom the
regime believes it can "remold" into "new socialist
men," rather than by the elders, who always commanded
respect in traditional China. In theory at least, revolutionary enthusiasm has become more important than
either experience or conventional wisdom, and mascu-
line energy more important, for both men and women,
than traditional manners or feminine charm.

Another fundamental change has been the spectacular
rise in the social prestige accorded the military. Contrary to popular myth, generals and soldiers, while given
a low social rating in China in the past, have always
been important in the Chinese scheme of things. But
it is true that they have not generally been honored or
accorded great respect. Now, however, things are very
different, and military men occupy a high position in
the scale of social esteem in China. In many respects,
it is legitimate to say that Chinese society under Communist rule has been militarized as it has been politicized.

The written and spoken Chinese language is also undergoing a revolutionary change. This change began
several decades ago, but it has been greatly accelerated
since 1949. Its long-range consequence is difficult to
estimate, but it will certainly be significant, since language and thought are so intimately related. Not only

is the vocabulary in common usage being transformed, as often happens in revolutionary situations, but the written language, which has played a peculiarly important role in the development and preservation of Chinese culture, is being deliberately altered.

To the Communists, the Chinese language is not essentially a vehicle for preserving China's history and traditional culture, as it was widely regarded in the past. It is merely a tool to be simplified, utilized, and manipulated in whatever ways seem pragmatically most desirable to foster the current revolution. The Chinese Communists' ultimate hope is to introduce a phonetic alphabet for general usage in place of the complicated traditional Chinese characters—a change that would be of immense significance. Their immediate, interim goal, toward which they have already made progress, is to simplify the existing characters so that they will be easier to learn and write; in this way, China's millions can rapidly be made literate and can be more effectively indoctrinated and trained to serve the purposes of the state.

Similarly, a new utilitarian and revolutionary philosophy of aesthetics motivates the Chinese Communists' approach to art and literature. Art is not for art's sake, but to serve the cause of revolution; like most aspects of life in Communist China today, it has been thoroughly politicized and proletarianized.

The Communists are also consciously attempting to foster entirely new patterns of social behavior and human relations in China. Perhaps the communization program introduced in 1958 revealed more clearly than anything else the image of the new society that at least

some of the Chinese Communist leaders hope to create.
It would be a society in which there would be the
greatest possible collective activity, even communal liv-
ing. It is true that Peking's recent tactical retreat from
the extreme policies of 1958 has involved many modifi-
cations of the radical measures that were promoted
when the communes were first introduced, but there is
no reason as yet to conclude that this marks the abandon-
ment of the Chinese Communists' ultimate goal of a
society in which not only the economy but social relations in general would be collectivized to the maximum
degree possible.

Underlying all these broad changes, and many others
that could be mentioned, has been the new Marxist-
Leninist-Stalinist-Maoist ideology, which provides the
driving force behind the entire Chinese Communist
revolution. This all-pervasive, state-supported ideology
has become a new orthodoxy in China, one that the
Chinese Communists insist should replace totally not
only traditional Confucian values but also the many
competing ideological forces that have penetrated China
from the West during the modern period.

The ideological revolution being pushed by the Chinese Communists involves much more, one should
hasten to point out, than merely formal indoctrination
in the basic tenets of the major Communist prophets—
dialectical materialism, class struggle, and all the rest.
It also demands a continuing effort to change many of
the most fundamental traditional values and attitudes
of the Chinese people.

The ideas of harmony, compromise, adjustment, and
stability, which have been so important in China in the

past, are anathema to the Communists. In their place, the new regime is trying to induce the Chinese people, especially the younger generation, to accept a very different set of values and attitudes, emphasizing struggle, change, progress, and innovation. "Work, study, and struggle"—these, above all, are the basic requirements for the good life in the Chinese Communists' scheme of things. These, together with other essentials such as iron discipline, self-sacrifice, acute class-consciousness, intense patriotism, heightened political awareness, and a strong collectivist outlook—plus, of course, technical skill—are the prerequisites for the "new socialist man" who is required to achieve their utopian blueprint of a future Communist society.

To observers who knew something of China before the Communist take-over, and who have continued to follow the course of the revolution there since 1949, what is perhaps most striking is the breakneck pace of the change that has been taking place in recent years, and the fact that the Chinese Communists have been able to sustain this pace for so long.

This is not meant to imply, by any means, that Peking's leaders have not encountered serious problems and resistance, or to suggest that their revolutionary drive to "remold" Chinese society in its entirety has not experienced notable setbacks as well as advances. In many fields, the course of events in recent years has followed an erratic pattern: There have been two steps forward, then one step back. In short, tactical retreats have followed strategic advances when the regime's abrupt moves forward have met intractable problems or deep-rooted resistance that could not be ignored.

One could cite a great many examples of such tactical retreats. In the early 1950's, Peking's attempt to implement its new marriage law at top speed, to "emancipate" China's women abruptly from ancient traditions whether they liked it or not, encountered such major difficulties in rural China that the Communists were forced to slow down temporarily and adopt a much more gradual approach to the problem. Almost all of the Communists' major moves to organize the peasantry, and to reorganize agriculture, have met significant resistance, and have been followed by tactical moves backward. Even today, the regime is still forced to acknowledge that China's peasants cling stubbornly to such "bourgeois" concepts as the desire to control their own plots of land. A large percentage of China's intellectual class inherited from the pre-Communist period have also proved to be extremely stubborn in clinging to many "bourgeois"—that is, non-Communist —ideas. Although the new regime has converted some of these intellectuals, and has had relatively little difficulty in controlling the others, it has learned the hard way that, despite repeated efforts at indoctrination, it is by no means easy to convert all of them.

But so far none of these problems has blocked the headlong process of revolutionary change in China. In fact, to date, none has even checked its great momentum for more than brief periods. In many areas of Chinese life, the pace of change has been maintained, and even accelerated, despite all the resistance deeply imbedded in Chinese culture. The recent setbacks resulting from the communization program may conceivably affect the pace of change more than other failures in the past, but this remains to be seen.

Some years ago, a foreigner who had just toured Communist China came out to Hong Kong and remarked, with awe in his voice: "I never thought that human beings and society could be reconstructed so easily." It is difficult to know, of course, what he really meant by the word "easily." If he meant that the changes of recent years had been relatively painless, he was very wrong. The plastic surgery that the Communists have been performing on Chinese society for over a decade has been painful indeed for millions of Chinese, in a psychic as well as a physical sense. The price in terms of economic austerity, overwork, rigid political control, and unprecedented regimentation has been extremely high. The entire twelve-year period since the Communist take-over has been one of almost continuous struggle, tension, and uncertainty in China, and these are not "easily" endured for a prolonged period of time.

But if, in using the word "easily," the visitor actually meant "rapidly," it is easy to share some of his awe. The Chinese Communists have dramatically demonstrated that an effective totalitarian regime can achieve extensive social change at a breakneck pace.

Does this fact have any relevance for our own concepts about the potentialities and the processes of change in the developing areas of the world? It has been pointed out that most of the agents of Western influence in the non-Western world have been largely unconscious of the fact that they have served as instruments of revolutionary change. In the past few years, however, this has changed to some degree, especially since the start of large-scale foreign economic-aid programs. Many of the major Western nations have begun to adopt policies consciously directed toward encouraging and supporting change, at least in the economic sphere, in a wide range of developing countries.

There appears to be a very great contrast, however, between certain of the basic assumptions underlying the majority of the development programs supported by Western nations and the assumptions upon which the Communists, in China and elsewhere, operate—especially those concerning the feasible and desirable rate of social change in developing countries. The West generally assumes that social change must be gradual and cautious, that it can only succeed if it builds slowly upon the basic "felt needs" of a majority of the ordinary people, and that programs must be formulated in such a way as to avoid, whenever possible, head-on clashes with the obvious obstacles to change strongly entrenched in all transitional societies. The Communists, on the other hand, often emphasize appeals to "felt needs" while they are still struggling for power, but once in power they shift gears and place prime emphasis on the most rapid possible rate of social change, directed toward goals they themselves define as desirable or necessary.

There are some obvious reasons for this contrast, reasons that are inherent in the differences between totalitarian and nontotalitarian regimes. The Communists' ideological dogmatism provides them with clear goals, and their totalitarian political philosophy sanctions the use of extreme coercion to achieve these goals.

But, examining the Chinese case, this is certainly not the entire explanation. Crude coercion is not the only element that has enabled the Chinese Communists to generate a process of extremely rapid social change—even though it has been a crucial element in the process, always present if not always apparent. But there have been other important elements, too: the revolutionary dynamism of the Chinese Communists' movement and their remarkable techniques for positively mobilizing people and resources, and for using organized social pressures to achieve their ends.

Examining the contrast, during the past decade and more, between the rapid rate of change in Communist China and the painfully slow pace of change in some of the developing non-Communist nations on its periphery, one can pose a number of questions that may need to be examined more seriously than they have been to date.

What will be the consequences in the long run if non-Communist countries, despite their growing internal pressures for change, lag dramatically behind Communist countries such as China in their modernization and development programs? Is a more rapid pace of social change not only desirable but also feasible in some of these non-Communist countries? Are there ways in which these countries can, in effect, force the pace of change by adopting more effective methods of social mobilization, mass persuasion, and even manipulation of social pressures, while still avoiding crudely coercive totalitarian methods and preserving a political system that permits the development of democratic institutions and values? There are no easy answers to questions such as these. Whatever the answers, however, it is virtually certain that the rapid pace of development and change in Communist China will exert a powerful influence on impatient revolutionaries in other non-Western countries, wherever and whenever the process of change in these countries lags seriously behind the pressures for change, thereby creating dangerous frustrations.

So far in this discussion, much has been said about the process of revolutionary change in China, and the word "continuity" has not even been mentioned. Perhaps it is clear by now, though, why the emphasis has been on change. When one looks at all that has taken place in a brief thirteen years in China, one is tempted to conclude that literally everything is in flux, and that the revolutionary upheaval is of such magnitude that the China of the future will bear almost no relation to the China of the past.

But is this a valid conclusion? Can even an upheaval such as the one now under way in China escape the past? Are all the changes now taking place likely to be permanent? To what extent may some of them really be less fundamental than might appear at first glance? Are there continuities with the past that can be identified even now, while the revolution is at its peak? Is it likely that others will become evident in the future? Questions such as these are easier to ask than to answer. But it is difficult to avoid asking them.

Perhaps it would be wise, right at the start, to examine some of the various possible meanings of the word "change." Change in relation to what? Change by comparison with traditional Chinese society as it existed before the impact of the West in the nineteenth century? Change merely by comparison with the abnormal chaos that existed in China on the eve of Communist take-over? Or change of such a fundamental sort that it represents a clear break with both traditional China and pre-1949 modern China? Whichever kind of change one has in mind, is it possible to identify underlying continuities with the past? Questions such as these may provide a framework for looking at the process of revolution in Communist China from several different perspectives.

Some of the "changes" listed in the brief inventory already made of developments since 1949 obviously fall into one general category: They are very similar to changes that have occurred periodically in China during the two millennia since the initial establishment of a Chinese empire. In a sense, such changes can easily be fitted into the Chinese dynastic cycle. For example, reunification of the Chinese empire and the re-establishment of a strong, highly centralized, expansionist central government, together with the suppression of political localism and regionalism, have been among the first aims, and the major accomplishments, of every important new Chinese dynasty. If one looked at these alone, therefore, one might be inclined to regard the Chinese Communist regime simply as a new dynasty. This is not meant to imply, of course, that changes in this general category are unimportant. They are actually of very great importance. They alone are sufficient to explain much about the tremendous difference between the China of today and the relatively weak, chaotic, and confused China of the recent past. But it is questionable to what extent such changes should be regarded as genuinely revolutionary. They are a part of the continuum of China's long history.

Some of the other changes listed earlier clearly fit into another category. They are without doubt revolutionary, in a very real sense, if one uses traditional China as a basis for comparison. But if one views them in the context of the century-old modern revolution in China, they are by no means entirely new. As indicated earlier, a start had been made, long before the Communists seized power, toward developing modern industry and commerce and establishing modern governmental institutions, and attempts had been made to introduce mass political organizations and to build modern military forces. Long before 1949, modern nationalism, patriotism, and many other new values had started to take root. Slowly but surely, important changes had begun to take place in China's class structure, in the role of the family, in the place of women in society, in the position of youth, and in the nature of the Chinese language, to cite only a few examples.

Many foreigners who visit Communist China today appear to be unaware of this, and they report virtually every innovation that they observe as being something totally new. Needless to say, they are encouraged to do this by the Chinese Communists themselves, who are now engaged in the task of carefully rewriting Chinese history and are eager to take credit for every significant move toward modernization that has ever taken place in China. But the continuity between current developments and China's recent revolutionary past is important, and it should not be overlooked.

At the same time, neither should it be exaggerated. Even though the first steps toward modernization in China were taken long before 1949, the Communists have accelerated the pace of change so greatly that what has occurred in recent years appears, in many instances, to bear little relation to what went on before 1949. The change in degree has in many instances been so great, in short, that it amounts virtually to a change in kind.

Many of the innovations that the Communists have introduced since 1949 represent a radical break with the Chinese past, whether ancient or modern. Often, the continuity one finds in these instances is with the Soviet, not the Chinese, past. The political apparatus that the Chinese Communists have established is the first genuinely totalitarian regime rooted in the Chinese masses. Many other innovations are extremely revolutionary: importation of a new total ideology; establishment of new political, social, and economic institutions; complete restructuring of the Chinese class system and economy; initiation of forced-draft economic development; collectivization and communization of society; adoption of new techniques for controlling and mobilizing the entire population; introduction of new Marxist values and goals; and attempts to create new patterns of social behavior and even a new national personality. These developments, unlike anything in Chinese history, link China to a new past, that of the world Communist movement.

However, if one is to attempt to understand both the

present and the future of China, there are further questions that need to be raised. Are there, for example, other elements of subtle continuity with China's past that help to explain the success of the Chinese Communist Party in establishing its rule? In asking this question, one does not need to imply any historical inevitability about the Chinese Communists' success, a view that was rejected earlier. Nor is it necessary to focus on general parallels between certain periods in Chinese history and the present, although such parallels are certainly of interest and are doubtless relevant to an understanding of Communist China. Some observers have pointed out parallels, for example, between the premodern authoritarianism of the short-lived Chin dynasty 2,000 years ago and the Chinese Communist regime, or between certain specific elements in the Chinese Communist program, such as land reform, and precedents in China's long past.

The question that may be most significant, however, is whether in the past there have been certain fundamental characteristics of Chinese society which, when China's initial brief experiment with parliamentary and democratic government failed, predisposed the Chinese to accept modern totalitarianism. Certainly, one can say that the dominant political tradition in China has been one of authoritarianism, centralization, and control. Did this provide a basis, after democracy had been discredited, for the establishment of modern Communism? There has also been a long history of ideological orthodoxy, conformity, and thought control, embodied for 2,000 years in Confucianism and neo-Confucianism. Did this tradition make it easier for the Chinese than it would have been for some others to accept a new ideological orthodoxy, Marxism-Leninism?

Throughout Chinese history, the individual has been subordinated to the group—first, and above all, the family, but also many other social groups. Is it possible that this tradition minimized the Chinese resistance to modern forms of collectivism that also place primary emphasis on the group, even though now various sorts of political organizations have usurped the role of the family and other traditional social institutions as the primary focus for group loyalty? In premodern China, there was a long tradition of government control of, and in some instances direct participation in, key sectors of the economy. Did this prepare the way for acceptance of modern state socialism?

One can also ask whether, despite the tremendous impact of the Soviet model and the great influence of imported ideas in China during the first decade of Communist rule, certain deep-rooted patterns of Chinese thought and behavior are likely to reassert themselves in the years ahead and to exert a more significant influence on the Chinese Communist regime. If so, could this produce a significantly variant form of Communism in China, one which, while it might continue to be an important part of what the Communists call their "socialist world system," might also become increasingly distinctive and Chinese in many respects? Is there already evidence of such a trend? For example, is the Chinese Communists' special emphasis on the potentialities of mobilized, organized masses of human labor in their economic development program (an emphasis that came to the fore most dramatically in the "great leap forward" and the communization policies) related in any way to the long tradition in China of large-scale, state-directed public works constructed with drafted labor? Is the unique stress placed on mass thought control by the Chinese Communists linked at all to traditional Chinese concepts about the nature and psychology of man, the importance of education and "self-cultivation," and the possibility of reconstructing human personality?

Many questions of this sort can be posed, but unfortunately few of them can be answered with confidence at present. Perhaps some are really unanswerable. On the other hand, we could probably make better educated guesses and substantially increase our understanding of China's past, present, and future if we had much greater knowledge and understanding than we do now of the complex interrelationships among three crucial elements: the current revolutionary developments in Communist China, the historical past out of which the Communist movement in China emerged, and the Soviet model that the Chinese Communists adopted at the start as their principal model. To acquire such knowledge and understanding, we need to draw increasingly upon the skills and talents of many different kinds of people: social scientists of many sorts, who are capable of analyzing the events now unfolding in China; Sovietologists, who can illuminate the meaning of the Russian experience in relation to China; and Sinologists and modern historians of China, who can throw increased light on the relationship between China's past and the current course of the Chinese revolution.

The character of Chinese society ten or twenty years

from now will certainly be different both from the traditional society of China and from the societies now emerging in other Communist countries with distinctive cultural and national traditions. And yet, at the same time, it will doubtless be a society that is strongly influenced both by the imported Communist theories and models that China's rulers now accept and by many unique traditions that are deeply imbedded in China's long history. What the exact mixture of these various influences will be is not easy to predict. One of the main tasks in the years immediately ahead, for those who attempt to understand the course of developments in China and to predict the emerging shape of the future, will be to analyze this mixture and to estimate what its results are likely to be.

III

PROBLEMS FOR
THE FUTURE

THERE ARE two different perspectives from which
one can examine China today and speculate about
the China of the future. If one focuses only on the
Chinese Communists' visible accomplishments during
the thirteen years since they came to power, it is very
clear that they have already made notable, and in some
cases spectacular, progress in certain fields. There is
little doubt, moreover, that in some of these fields they
are likely to continue making important gains toward
their basic goals in the decade ahead.

If, on the other hand, one focuses solely on their problems and failures, the perspective is rather different.
The Chinese Communists have encountered many serious difficulties already—some of these, too, have been
fairly spectacular—and more than a few of their problems raise important questions that must be examined
if one is attempting to estimate what Communist rule
is likely to mean for the Chinese people, and for the
rest of the world, in the years to come. Any analysis of
Communist China that concentrates on only one of these
perspectives—on either successes and accomplishments

or failures and problems—cannot avoid being distorted
or misleading.

To obtain a general view of the present Peking regime, it is necessary to examine, at least briefly, a few
of the Chinese Communists' accomplishments *and* problems in a variety of fields: industrialization and urbani-
zation; demographic trends and policies; the role of the
peasants and agriculture; possible political trends in the
future under the Chinese Communists' so-called "democratic dictatorship"; China's continuing development
as a modern military power; and the growth of China's
influence in international affairs and its meaning for all
of us. This is obviously a big order, and it will not be
possible to do more than mention the most significant
accomplishments or problems in each of these fields.

Industrialization is a good starting point, since it is
one of the basic goals of the Communist regime in
China. This is the field, moreover, in which the Chinese
Communists have, without doubt, made their greatest
gains to date. It is also the field in which their accomplishments are most visible—and most impressive, both
to the Chinese and to foreign visitors. In many respects,
industrialization has been enshrined by the Communists
as the prime symbol of modernization and national
power in China, as it has also been in more than a few
of the other developing countries, and the Peking regime has pursued its industrialization goals with remarkable energy and singleness of purpose.

The industrial base that the Communists inherited
when they seized power in China was extremely small
and highly localized. It consisted primarily of the limited number of heavy industries that the Japanese had

constructed in Manchuria, plus a few textile and other light consumer-goods industries, built mainly by foreign capital, in coastal cities such as Shanghai and Tientsin. Even these few industries were operating at extremely low levels of output. This was certainly not an impressive starting point. China's industrial base in 1949 was much smaller, for example, than that inherited by the Bolsheviks from the Czarist regime in 1917.

Almost immediately, however, the Chinese Communists set about the task of organizing, mobilizing, and allocating the resources of the nation to work toward their ultimate aim of building a fully industrialized state. At first, they concentrated on a limited objective —rehabilitation of China's small existing industrial base. During 1950–52, now labeled the "period of reconstruction," they were largely successful in getting existing factories back into operation, repairing transport lines, reviving domestic trade, and controlling inflation—all of which laid the groundwork for a planned national development program.

Then, in 1953, Peking announced its first Five-Year Plan and started the job of building new industries. Rapidly, industrialism spread to many areas of the country, including remote interior provinces that had hardly been touched by modernization before. And new products, never manufactured in China in the past, started coming off Chinese production lines. Patterned on the Stalinist model, China's first Plan called for over-all state planning, socialization, and high levels of state investment—all of which were designed to enforce consumer austerity and channel the nation's resources and energies into the building of new industries at the fastest possible rate.

From the start, the Chinese Communists placed prime emphasis upon the development of heavy industries: iron, steel, coal, electricity, machine tools, chemicals, transport equipment, and the like. Their basic aim was to produce machines to produce more machines to produce still more machines. The fundamental goal, in short, was to build for the future rather than to meet the immediate consumer needs of the Chinese people.

With this concentration of effort, the rate of industrial and over-all growth that the Chinese Communists soon achieved was very impressive. It was far above the rate of growth in the majority of underdeveloped nations, and most of it was growth of a kind that contributed directly to the enhancement of China's industrial power. During 1953–57, for example, the annual output of many of China's basic heavy industries doubled or tripled. Total industrial production, it was claimed, rose by nearly 120 per cent. And China's gross national product increased at an average annual rate of perhaps 7 or 8 per cent. In terms of the Chinese Communists' own priority goals—particularly the goal of industrial progress—the first Plan was clearly an over-all success.

By the end of the Plan, however, there were signs that the industrialization program might be losing some of its momentum. The terminal year, 1957, was a difficult one. Soviet aid dropped off; China's new collectives were encountering difficulties; and Peking was forced to retrench in many fields. To meet this situation, the Chinese Communist leaders adopted radical new measures

in 1958, most notably their so-called "great leap forward" and communization program.

Determined not only to check the seeming loss of
momentum in 1957, but to step up substantially the
pace of economic growth in China, Peking's leaders
recklessly threw away the book, so to speak, and attempted to achieve almost total mobilization of man-
power and other resources in order to accelerate their
rate of development. They projected new rates of
growth unprecedented in China or anywhere else. The
key to this new approach was the assumption that man-
power plus ideological fervor could achieve miracles,
and in the industrial field the Chinese Communists
attempted to supplement their program for building
large-scale modern industries with a program to develop
thousands of small-scale rural industries using a maximum of labor and a minimum of capital.

For a brief period after the start of the "great leap,"
Communist China did experience an outburst of organized human activity that probably has few parallels
in history, at any time or in any place. But clearly the
Chinese Communists attempted to do too much too
fast, and they made some very serious mistakes. Economic planning and administration, in effect, broke
down. Many of the new economic experiments were
failures; notable among these were the much-publicized
"backyard steel furnaces" and other hastily promoted
rural industries. After being worked to the point of
exhaustion, and organized to the point where they were
deprived of almost all individual incentives, the Chinese
people began to react in the only way that they could—
by dragging their feet.

All in all, the "great leap," while it did result in spectacular advances in certain fields, created as many problems as it solved, and before long the Chinese Communists were forced to start retreating from both the "great leap" policies and the accompanying communization program. They are still, in fact, in retreat, and today the Communists' entire economic program in China is undergoing a period of shakedown and uncertainty. The regime is trying to catch its breath and get things back on an even keel.

This is an especially difficult period, therefore, in which to look into the future. Reliable data are lacking even for the present situation. The Chinese Communists, for example, did not publish any over-all economic statistics in either 1960 or 1961. In fact, during 1961 they did not even publish a general economic plan for the year.

Currently, Communist China's industrialization program appears to be stalled. Many factories have had to close down for varying periods of time for reorganization and repairs. And new construction seems to have been cut to a minimum. The Chinese economy is in a slump that could last for two to three years. But it would be self-delusion to project the present situation very far into the future—or, for that matter, to underestimate what has been accomplished in the recent past.

Despite all the failures of the "great leap," Communist China did make a dramatic, albeit brief, spurt forward in certain industrial fields during 1958–60. It is particularly relevant to note what happened in the steel industry, which the Peking regime pushed especially hard because of its fundamental importance to modern industrial power. Prior to the Communist take-over, China's steel output had never reached 1 million tons. By 1952, it had risen from its low starting point to 1.35 million tons. By the end of Communist China's first Five-Year Plan period, in 1957, it had quadrupled and stood at approximately 5.35 million tons. By 1960, despite setbacks in many fields after the "great leap," and despite the general economic confusion in China during 1959 and 1960, Peking claimed—and its claims may not have been too far off the mark in this case—that its steel output had soared to well over 18 million tons. There is no denying that this was a very impressive achievement, one that provided convincing evidence that the Chinese Communists are determined to build the industrial foundation for modern world power whatever the difficulties or costs. Even in the field of small industries, it would be a mistake to concentrate solely on the dramatic failures of the "great leap" and overlook the fact that, despite recent cutbacks, Communist China now has substantially more small-scale industries than before 1958.

It seems highly probable, if one can look beyond the present, that the Peking regime will weather its current economic crisis, that eventually there will be an upturn in the situation, and that as soon as they believe it to be feasible, the Chinese Communists will start once again to push forward in their industrialization program.

Several other things seem probable as well. The current slowdown in Peking's program to build heavy industries, even if it lasts as long as two to three years, is likely to be only temporary. After a shakedown period, the Chinese Communists, whatever the difficulties, will probably resume their drive toward industrial power, and it is certainly possible that before very many years have passed China may become the third most important world producer (in absolute, not per capita, terms) of key industrial products basic to modern power, surpassing nations such as Britain and Japan. (There is little prospect in the foreseeable future, however, that it will approach the output levels of the United States or the Soviet Union, even in the few basic industries to which it assigns top priority.)

The industrial map of China also seems destined to continue undergoing major changes. Actually, it has already changed greatly, even in the relatively brief period since the Communists came to power. New industrial centers have begun to develop in many areas of interior China, and they can be expected to continue growing. It is already evident where many of the major new urban industrial centers of China will be: Paotow, in Inner Mongolia; Hankow, in central China; Taiyuan, in north China; Lanchow, in northwest China; and Chungking, in southwest China.

Accompanying the growth of large-scale industrial centers, there may well be a continuing effort to develop vast numbers of small-scale industries in Communist China. In spite of the recent failures and setbacks in many such industries, a program to foster certain types of labor-intensive enterprises makes a good deal of economic sense in an overpopulated country such as China, and the Chinese Communists appear to have a deep and genuine faith that great things can be accomplished primarily through mass mobilization of human labor.

It seems highly unlikely at the moment, however, that the growth of rural industry in China in the years immediately ahead will be anything comparable to the development of the large-scale modern industries that symbolize national power in the Chinese Communists' eyes.

While it appears virtually certain that the Chinese Communists will resume their industrialization drive once there is any sign of a real economic upturn after the current slump, it seems almost equally certain that the difficulties they will encounter in this drive will multiply rather than decrease during the next few years. Two of the most fundamental problems they will face are the steady growth of population and the persistent lag in agriculture—both of which will be discussed briefly below. In addition, they are likely to face a growing problem in their international balance of payments, which will make it more difficult than in the past to import the capital goods required for further industrial expansion.

Today, Communist China is not receiving any long-term financial assistance from the Soviet Union for its development program, and it is experiencing real strain in its efforts to pay back debts already incurred. It is also forced to use much of its precious foreign-exchange reserves to purchase grain, rather than machines, from the West. One of the Chinese Communists' prime problems in the immediate future, therefore, is likely to be how to extract a sufficient surplus from the agricultural sector of China's economy to repay its past foreign debts and to pay for new capital-goods imports. As a consequence, they will probably feel under in-

creasing pressure to squeeze China's already hard-
pressed peasants to the maximum degree to support
their drive to acquire industrial power. In view of this
fact, the recent loosening of controls in the countryside
may prove to be no more than a brief tactical retreat.

In the light of these various factors, what will industrialization of the kind that the Chinese Communists
have been fostering mean for the Chinese people, especially the rural masses who make up a majority of
China's population, during the years immediately
ahead? Will Communist China, even if it is successful
in building a substantial base of heavy industry, become a fully industrialized, urbanized country in the
sense that nations such as Britain and Japan are? Or is
it more likely that while large islands of modern industry may grow in many parts of China, they may continue to be surrounded, for many years to come, by a
huge sea of relatively backward, nonindustrialized agriculture? Will the gap between urban and rural China
actually be narrowed, or will the regime be forced to
build its industry on the peasants' blood, sweat, and
tears, siphoning off the product of their labor and contributing relatively little to them in return?

The answers to such questions will depend in large
part upon the specific kind of industrialization policies
that the Chinese Communist leaders decide to push during the next few years. If they were to place increased
emphasis upon the need to satisfy consumer demands,
the gap between urban and rural China might slowly
be reduced. If, however—as seems more likely when one
looks beyond the present period of tactical retreat—they
persist in stressing the development of heavy industry

above all else, China may speedily build a strong industrial base for power, but the mass of China's population may not reap substantial benefit from this development for a long time to come. Instead of rapidly becoming a fully industrialized society, China may first become a nation in which impressive centers of modern industry grow by exploiting the relatively backward rural hinterland surrounding them.

It remains to be seen, in fact, whether Communist China will even become urbanized to any really significant degree in the years immediately ahead. There is no doubt that China's urban population will grow substantially, but it is conceivable that the rural population may also continue to grow almost as rapidly. During the first Five-Year Plan period, despite the rapid growth of heavy industries, China's cities were able to absorb only a small portion of the increase in China's total population. According to one estimate, while the urban population of China increased from approximately 77 million to 92 million during 1953–57, the rural population jumped from perhaps 510 million to 550 million, resulting in a five-year increase in the ratio of urban to total population of only a little over 1 per cent. By the end of the Plan, according to this estimate, Communist China, although it had built a great many new industries and had absorbed 15 million new persons into its cities, was still over 85 per cent rural.

The over-all growth of population in China poses some baffling conundrums about the future of what is already the most populous nation on earth. Demographic statistics are as incomplete as all other data on recent trends in Communist China, but most Western analysts now tend to accept Peking's 1953 census figure of over 580 million as a rough base line, and they seem to agree that the net increase in China's population since then has been either a little above or a little below 2 per cent a year. If these figures are even close to the truth, Communist China's population is now somewhere between 650 and 700 million. And if current trends continue, by the 1980's the population will reach the incredible figure of 1 billion. The possible consequences of such a population explosion, both for China's domestic program and for its attitudes toward the outside world, are difficult to conceive.

To date, Communist China's leaders have not even begun to face up to their population problem. It is true that for a brief period following the 1953 census they did give limited encouragement to certain types of birth control, but before long both their Marxist and their Chinese prejudices against limiting population reasserted themselves, and proposals for a birth-control program in China not only failed to receive official support but came under strong political attack. During the "great leap" period, Chinese Communist leaders actually declared that China was suffering from a shortage of labor. Amazingly enough, in a sense they were correct, at that particular moment in time. The "great leap," with its total mobilization of labor and its excessive demands upon the entire population, did create a temporary shortage of workers in China. But this was a highly artificial situation; the degree of mobilization that took place in that period was impossible to sustain.

Whatever attitude the regime adopts in the future, there will be no easy escape from the population prob-

lem in Communist China. It is conceivable that if the
Communists eventually were to recognize that they have
a problem, they might be able to achieve some measure
of success in promoting birth control through their
remarkable skill at manipulating and controlling people
by totalitarian methods. But the danger is that they will
continue refusing even to acknowledge the problem.
Thus, the inexorable growth of China's population
could result in a steady build-up of dangerous pressures
not only on China's vast peasant population—which,
both directly and indirectly, will bear the major burden
of supporting the regime's industrialization program—
but possibly also on the relatively underpopulated, food-
surplus areas that lie on its periphery, especially to the
south.

Many of the most important and baffling questions
about the future in Communist China relate, ultimately, to the question of what will happen to the
peasantry and to the entire agricultural sector of the
economy. Here the picture is quite different from that
in the field of industry. The accomplishments are far
less impressive, and the problems for the future loom
much larger.

Actually, no Communist regime anywhere, including
the Soviet one, has been really successful in dealing
with the problems posed by the peasantry and agriculture. The Chinese Communist regime is no exception.
The problems they have encountered are numerous
and basic: the problem of applying planning to agriculture; the problem of controlling the peasants while
attempting to stimulate them to greater productive
efforts; the problem of collectivizing the peasants and

overcoming their "bourgeois tendencies" (their desire, above all, to own land) ; the problem of siphoning off the existing agricultural surplus, yet somehow raising over-all agricultural output sufficiently to support a broad economic development program. These and many other problems have plagued almost all Communist regimes, and they plague Communist China today.

It is ironic, but nevertheless true, that the Communists' entire relationship with China's peasant population has fundamentally changed in the years since 1949. When the Chinese Communist Party was still struggling for power, pursuing a strategy of building rural revolutionary bases and forming a peasant army, it evolved highly successful land-reform policies that were designed to, and actually did, attract peasant support.

Since they came to power, however, and shifted their principal emphasis to industrialization, the Chinese Communists have been steadily compelled to increase their controls over the peasantry and to do everything possible to extract the available surplus from the agricultural sector of the economy. Soon after they had completed their land-reform program, which was implemented for the most part between 1950 and 1953, they initiated a big push toward collectivization, during 1955–56. This was followed in 1958 by communization. With the steady increase in state controls, the peasants —many of whom at the start were without doubt among the strongest supporters of the Chinese Communist revolutionary movement—have increasingly become the victims rather than the beneficiaries of the regime's economic development program.

The entire agricultural sector of the economy in China, moreover, has lagged seriously behind the rest of the regime's over-all development program. During the first Plan period, some progress was made, and grain output reportedly rose from roughly 154 million to perhaps 185 million tons. Despite this increase, however, the rate of over-all agricultural growth even in this early period was probably not very much above the rate of population growth. And during the past three years, events on the agricultural front have been almost calamitous. In 1958, the first year of the "great leap," the weather was good, and grain output did jump from 185 million to about 200–210 million tons—a not unimpressive increase. But then, in 1959, it dropped to perhaps 190 million, and in 1960 it may have been back at the 1957 level of 185 million. In 1961, there was little, if any, improvement, and the prospects for 1962 are uncertain. All the while, China's population has been steadily growing, and during this three-year period it may have increased by 30 to 40 million. Clearly, on the agricultural front, China is now further from achieving many of its basic goals than it was prior to the "great leap" and communization.

There are numerous explanations for the recent setbacks. The occurrence of serious natural disasters for three years in succession, starting in 1959, has certainly been a contributing factor. But this is by no means the whole explanation. Probably the major cause has been passive resistance to communization on the part of the peasants. In addition, the Chinese Communist regime itself has made some very great policy errors, such as indiscriminate pushing of techniques like "close planting" and "deep plowing," and these can be assigned a significant share of the blame.

However one analyzes the causes, there is no question that 1961 was an extremely difficult year in China, perhaps the most difficult year economically since the Communists assumed power. It was a year of widespread malnutrition, even though the available food was spread over the entire country to keep starvation to a minimum. It was also a year of severe shortages of agricultural raw materials and export products, shortages that helped to produce the general slowdown of Communist China's entire development program.

As a result of the situation that has been developing since 1959, the Chinese Communists have been forced to retreat substantially from both their communization program and a great many of the other agricultural policies promoted during the "great leap" period. This retreat has somewhat eased the pressures on China's peasantry. In time, this easing, plus good weather, will probably result in some sort of an upturn in agricultural production. But a real solution of the basic agricultural problems in China—particularly the problem of increasing per-acre output—will not be easily achieved. The need is for a considerably higher level of investment in agriculture (especially an increase in the use of chemical fertilizers), for general improvement in agricultural technology, and for further steps to provide increased incentives for the peasants.

The recent trends in Chinese Communist policies point in these directions, but it is by no means certain that they will prove to be more than temporary expedients. While one might argue that such steps are essential to provide a sound basis for future industrialization, it is clear that they would tend to slow down the rate of industrial development in the short run. And it is for this reason that the impatient leaders of Communist China may well be reluctant to review them as more than temporary. It seems highly possible that the Chinese Communists' overriding urge to press forward at top speed to build large-scale heavy industries will reassert itself before very long, and that when it does, this will result once again in a tightening of controls and in renewed attempts to manipulate the peasants, as soon as the top leaders in the regime think it is practicable. Perhaps Communist China's leaders have learned, since 1958, that there are limits beyond which the peasants cannot be pushed without diminishing returns. It seems improbable, however, that they have yet altered their basic priorities, except for tactical purposes.

Looking to the future, the most likely prospect is for a continuing seesaw contest between the regime and the peasantry—a contest that will probably involve severe tensions between a government driven to increase its controls and pressures on agriculture in order to pursue its industrial goals, and a peasant population that can be expected to continue resisting excessive controls and pressures, even if only by dragging their feet.

Despite all these problems, however, it is probable that farm output in China will slowly increase. But it seems equally probable that the increases will be far less than the regime desires and needs, and that the continued lag in agriculture will be one of the most basic and serious problems confronting the regime for a long time to come.

The many problems, tensions, and dilemmas—or, to use Mao Tse-tung's word, "contradictions"—created by fundamental economic problems are certain to affect the future political character of the Chinese Communist regime.

Today, Communist China is still ruled by its first generation of revolutionary leaders, men who came to power after long years of close association in a bitter guerrilla struggle. In many respects, the political apparatus they have established has been remarkably effective to date in carrying out the will of the Chinese Communist Party. The top leaders have maintained a unity unparalleled by that of any other Communist Party in the world. They have shown, on the one hand, intense dedication to their revolutionary goals and, on the other, notable flexibility in formulating and implementing their major policies. Although they have periodically resorted to extreme violence to enforce the Party's will, at the same time they have developed distinctive and remarkably effective methods of mass persuasion and manipulation and have relied heavily upon them.

What is likely to happen when a second generation of leaders takes over in Communist China, particularly if the problems and tensions briefly described above grow rather than decrease? Will new leaders be less doctrinaire and more willing to adjust the pace of development if they encounter serious difficulties? Or will they become more bureaucratic, less flexible, and even more callous in their choice of means to work toward their ends? Will they be more, or less, inclined to use coercion, rather than persuasion, in dealing with the Chinese people?

What will happen when Mao passes out of the picture? Will tensions increase within the top Chinese leadership? Even during recent years, there have been hints of important debates between two groups of leaders in China—labeled by some outsiders as the "radicals" and the "moderates"—but, under Mao's aegis, existing differences have been kept remarkably under control. When Mao's dominating personality passes from the scene, however, will this situation change?

The raising of such questions should not be interpreted as meaning, or even implying, that the Chinese Communists are on the verge of a major internal political crisis. One of the most remarkable aspects of the Communist regime in China during recent years has been its ability to prevent the development of serious internal schisms, and it appears today as if Mao has already made more careful preparations for an orderly succession of power at the time of his death than any other Communist leader has ever attempted. Nevertheless, questions of this sort deserve to be carefully examined.

There is really no basis for making confident predictions about what will take place when the next generation of leaders takes over in China, but it is possible to question whether the trend will necessarily be toward a slackening of ideological fervor, increased moderation and flexibility, and greater political liberalization, as some observers have suggested. It is quite conceivable, in fact, that the second generation of leaders in Communist China might be equally driven by the desire to build national power as rapidly as possible, and at the same time might be even less sensitive than the present leadership in taking popular sentiment into account, less flexible in adapting their policies as new problems arise, and less restrained in the use of coercive methods of rule. In short, if the pressures generated by internal problems were to increase, it is conceivable that the Chinese Communist regime under second-generation leaders might become more rather than less repressive, politically.

If one could look far enough into the future to envision a Chinese Communist regime that had already achieved many of its basic national goals, had begun to shift the emphasis of its economic program from building industrial power to satisfying the most urgent consumer needs of its population, and had also started to lose its militant revolutionary fervor, then one could imagine a process in China comparable to that which has been taking place in the Soviet Union since the death of Stalin. But there is little to suggest that this will happen soon. Not only is the revolution in China passing through a stage very different from the one that the Soviet Union has now entered, but the problems it faces are intrinsically more difficult, in many respects, than those met by the Russians even in the early years of the Bolshevik Revolution. As an overpopulated nation starting its development program from a minimum industrial base, Communist China faces a particularly long and hard struggle to achieve its goals, and because this struggle will inevitably encounter serious internal problems and pressures, the prospects for significant political liberalization in the near future seem slim indeed.

The organizational apparatus the Chinese Communists have built is a remarkable instrument of totalitarian rule, designed to translate the policies—whatever they may be—adopted by a handful of Party leaders at the top into effective action by the masses of China's huge population. The most radical political innovation in China since 1949, in fact, is not the reorganization of central political institutions at the national level, but the development, under Communist Party control and direction, of a vast network of Party, government, military, and mass political organizations that penetrates every sector of society and impinges directly upon the daily lives of ordinary people throughout the country.

The Communist Party itself, which has created and controls this apparatus, is a mass organization that operates on the lowest as well as the highest levels of society. Its disciplined members are closely controlled from the center through a tightly organized hierarchy operating under principles of "democratic centralism," yet at the same time they pursue a "mass line" that brings them into direct contact with the population as a whole. At every level, right down to the level of the individual factory and village, Party members represent the ultimate authority of the regime, occupy the leading positions in governmental, military, and mass political organizations, and provide the motive power that ensures the implementation of policies decided upon by the Party's Central Committee and Politburo.

The Party's outreach is made effective through a variety of other organizations that directly involve millions of non-Party people in the control apparatus of the regime. The government, which, in a sense, is merely an administrative instrument for implementing the Party's decisions, extends its mandate to the lowest levels through many channels. A hierarchy of local congresses

and councils mobilizes wide participation in government affairs. A nationwide civil-police organization
maintains an effective public-security system (especially
in the cities) that is in close contact not only with resi-
dents' committees and various sorts of mass organizations, but also with most of the population. At various
periods, special security committees have played an important role in rooting out sources of disaffection. The
courts are highly political organs that have generally
placed more emphasis on implementing Party policies
and "educating" the people than on defending individual rights or stabilizing the *status quo*. A national
system of procurators is responsible for investigating
violations of law and order; its members serve also as
prosecutors for the state. In addition, personnel in the
government's own supervision or control apparatus
check on the functioning of the state apparatus itself.
Secret-police units, operating under both the Party and
the government, are less important in China than in
other Communist-ruled states, but they nevertheless
exist and reinforce the regime's over-all system of
control.

Economic organizations, established and directed by
the state, also enmesh everyone in the regime's apparatus. Virtually the entire population of China now
belongs to institutions that fit directly into the state
economic bureaucracy. In rural areas, the communes—
which have merged governmental and economic functions—and their many subsidiary organizations are all-
encompassing. The industrial labor force in urban areas
is grouped into unions that are really mass political
organizations, rather than unions in the non-Communist

sense of the word. Government-directed state trading agencies and cooperatives control domestic as well as foreign commerce. And, of course, rationing of basic economic necessities is an extremely effective instrument of political control.

The military system also reaches to the lowest levels of society and plays an important role in the apparatus of Chinese Communist rule. Units of public-security troops are stationed at strategic points throughout the country. And millions of peasants have been organized into local militia forces, whose purposes appear to be as much political as military.

These various instruments of control are merely one aspect, however, of the Communists' political system in China. Of equal, and perhaps even greater, importance are the instruments for positive organization, mobilization, and indoctrination of the masses. The Chinese Communists have placed unusual emphasis on techniques of "coercive persuasion." They have propagandized the entire population and have subjected a large portion of it to intensive "thought reform." All media for expressing and communicating ideas are utilized to disseminate both the basic ideology of the regime and the current Party line on every matter of any importance. Indoctrination in small groups has been developed to a fine art. And the regular educational system has been transformed so that it serves as a primary channel for imposing the regime's new ideological orthodoxy upon the people.

In addition to all of this, a complex web of mass political organizations under Communist control serves as one of the most effective channels for mobilizing the

Chinese people. Established on a nationwide basis for almost every identifiable group in the population— peasants, laborers, women, youth, students, former businessmen, intellectuals, artists, writers, scientists—these organizations hold frequent meetings, constantly indoctrinate their members, and, especially during special mass campaigns initiated by Peking, mobilize them to take an active part in a wide range of activities.

This political apparatus has now become so firmly established in Communist China that the possibility of an organized opposition taking shape, even when there is widespread dissatisfaction—as there clearly has been in recent years—has been reduced to a minimum. Only if the apparatus itself were to begin to split apart would the possibility of effective organized opposition become real, and there is no sign to date that this has begun to happen.

In the post–"great leap" slump, there has been some evidence, for the first time, of a noticeable decline of fervor and a loosening of discipline among some lower-level cadres within the system. There have also been signs, in recent years, of an almost inevitable process of increasing bureaucratization. These trends are significant. If the regime is unable to check them, they will certainly affect the efficiency with which the apparatus operates. But there is no basis for believing that, in the near future, they are likely to have any very significant effect on the essential nature of the system or on the basic policies that the regime will pursue.

Whatever domestic policies the Chinese Communist leaders adopt in the next few years, one can be fairly certain that a constant, persistent motive underlying most of what they do will be the desire to build China into a strong, modern world power. This goal has been, and will certainly continue to be, a basic one in the shaping of both their domestic programs and their foreign policy.

Nationalism has reached a new peak under Communist rule in China—a fact that is more than slightly ironic if one recalls the strong antinationalism of the early followers of Marx—and, not surprisingly, the Chinese Communists have devoted great energy to the development of military power.

In the military sphere, as in many others, Communist China has made notable progress during the past thirteen years, but if one looks to the future, there are serious problems ahead for China as well as the rest of the world.

The Peking regime's major military accomplishments to date are fairly well known, and perhaps do not need great elaboration here. In a little over a decade, the Chinese Communists have converted their original revolutionary guerrilla forces into one of the strongest conventional armies in the world. Reorganized, modernized, and re-equipped during the Korean War, Peking's army, consisting now of about 2.5 million men, is second in size only to that of the Soviet Union; the Korean War dispelled whatever doubts may have existed up to that time about its effectiveness and ability to fight. The Chinese Communists' air force, built entirely since 1949, has never been fully tested in combat, and some questions can be raised about its present quality; but with 2,500 planes (mostly jets), it is clearly a major, second-rank air force, the largest in Asia, and it cannot be lightly dismissed in any calculations of Communist China's new military power.

The existence of this modernized Chinese military machine has already had a sizable impact on world affairs, in subtle as well as obvious ways. Ever since the Korean War, the possibility of mass Chinese intervention in crisis situations on China's periphery has imposed definite restraints upon the West's willingness and ability to exert its influence in these areas. Instead of being a power vacuum, as in the past, China under Communist rule now casts a long shadow, and exerts a strong influence, over many of its neighbors. Recent events in Laos—to cite just one example—might have been far different if Chinese power had not been an element that could not be ignored in the military equation.

But Communist China's military power is by no means unlimited, and Peking's leaders are fully aware of this fact. Knowing it, and being realists, they have not—as some observers seem to have assumed—acted with complete recklessness or irresponsible abandon, even in areas directly adjacent to mainland China. Actually, in many situations, they have so far exercised considerable self-control and even caution, pushing and probing to test the West's intentions and determination, but drawing back whenever the risks of major military conflict have appeared to outweigh the possible gains from using military threats and pressures.

The most obvious limitation on the Chinese Communists' ability to make China's power effectively felt abroad, even in Asia, is, of course, their lack of an independent nuclear capacity. It has been Peking's lack of

nuclear weapons that, above all else, has imposed severe
limits, for example, on its ability to challenge the
United States directly in situations involving real risks
of major war, such as the successive crises in the Taiwan
Strait.

From the viewpoint of leaders such as those in Peking
—who not only aspire, in general terms, to major-power
status, but are determined to work specifically toward
the recovery of Taiwan and the elimination of Ameri-
can power from the Western Pacific—the acquisition of
an independent nuclear capacity is unquestionably a
major aim. But for a country such as China, still in the
early stages of economic development, this is an aim
that poses major problems.

The Soviet Union has not been willing to provide
Communist China with full backing for its desire to
join the so-called "nuclear club." It is true that Moscow
has given Peking some support in the field of nuclear
energy. For example, it has provided at least one research reactor, as well as supplies of enriched uranium
to operate it. And, in certain situations, such as the
offshore-islands crisis of 1958, the Soviet Union has
backed Communist China with threats (carefully quali-
fied) to use Soviet nuclear weapons in retaliation against
any Western attempts to use them against China. But
the Russian policy has seemed to be one of providing no
more—even in the field of nuclear energy for peaceful
purposes—than the minimum assistance required to preserve the Sino-Soviet alliance. There have been more
than a few hints, in fact, that the Russians have been far
from enthusiastic about the prospect of Communist
China's acquiring nuclear weapons. And as Sino-Soviet

relations have deteriorated, especially during the past two years, the Russians have doubtless become even more unwilling to help the Chinese Communists become a nuclear power.

But Peking seems determined, nevertheless, to join the nuclear club, with or without outside backing. In 1958, a top Chinese Communist military leader openly declared that his nation plans to manufacture its own nuclear weapons in due time, and it has doubtless been working toward this goal ever since. There is little question that it will eventually be able to achieve at least the first steps toward this end. According to one careful estimate, for example, even if the Chinese Communists rely solely upon the output of the one research reactor known to be operating near Peking, they conceivably might be able to build and explode their first nuclear device by mid-1963.

At the same time, however, there are indications that in their over-all military planning at present the Chinese Communists may well be proceeding on the assumption that they will not possess a significant deliverable nuclear capacity for some time to come. These facts may not actually be as contradictory as they might appear on the surface. Possibly, the Chinese Communists' immediate aim in the nuclear-weapons field is a rather limited one: simply to enter the nuclear club in a symbolic sense. This they could do merely by exploding a nuclear device. The real military significance of such an accomplishment might well be limited, since a considerable period of time would then be needed for Communist China to develop a usable nuclear arsenal, but the immediate psychological impact of even one nuclear explosion in China would doubtless be profound throughout Asia—and on world affairs in general.

If and when Communist China does acquire even a token nuclear capacity, will it then become increasingly militant, and increasingly willing to take risks to achieve its major foreign-policy aims? This remains to be seen. But it is certainly not impossible. Communist China's leaders might conclude that once they possess even a token nuclear capacity—a nuclear fuse with which they could threaten to trigger major nuclear war—this would immediately and significantly enhance their ability to make their voice heard in world affairs.

One should hasten to add, however, that it would be a great mistake to assume that the Chinese Communists regard military conflict as the only, or even the principal, instrument with which to pursue their struggle for world-power status and the expansion of their international influence. Actually, their foreign-policy arsenal is an extremely varied one. Conventional diplomacy, trade, aid, cultural diplomacy, the support of subversion abroad—these and other instruments of foreign policy all play important roles in Communist China's struggle to achieve its major aims.

But there is no doubt that the Chinese Communists are extraordinarily sensitive to shifts in what they call the "world balance of forces." And it would be surprising, indeed, if they did not attempt to exploit to the full any developments that appeared to strengthen their hand in international affairs. There is little doubt, for example, that one of the underlying causes of growing Sino-Soviet tensions since 1957 has been an important difference between Peking and Moscow in their views on the world power balance, the risks of war, and their implications for Communist-bloc strategy. Apparently, after the Soviets had launched their first Sputnik and ICBM in 1957, the Chinese Communists concluded that the entire Communist bloc should move rapidly and decisively to exploit the strategic advantage that Mao believed these technological breakthroughs provided. But the Russians, sensitive to the risks of nuclear war, were more cautious.

Contrary to the interpretation of some observers, the Chinese Communists during this period have not been actually advocating major nuclear war. They have, however, been urging that the entire Communist bloc be willing to take larger risks of war in order to push toward its basic objectives, including, of course, China's own major objectives.

There is another fact that cannot be ignored if one attempts to look to the future. Communist China, without any doubt, is today the most frustrated of all the world's leading powers. It is the only major power, for example, that still has important unfulfilled territorial claims. It is also the only one denied general recognition and acceptance into the major international councils. Intense frustration is probably a major cause, in fact, of Communist China's recent militancy. Would increased frustration lead the Chinese Communists toward greater recklessness in the future? This is difficult to predict with certainty, but there is no denying that it might be possible.

One of the most significant recent developments in international affairs has been the visible deterioration of relations between Communist China and the Soviet

Union, and one of the most important questions for the future is whether the Sino-Soviet alliance will continue intact or whether the two partners will split.

When the Chinese Communists first came to power, they consciously decided, as Mao Tse-tung put it, to "lean to one side." The Sino-Soviet Treaty of Friendship, Alliance, and Mutual Assistance, signed in 1950, became the cornerstone of Peking's foreign policy, and the Chinese Communists completely reoriented their trade and other economic relations away from the West and toward the Soviet bloc. China's first Five-Year Plan was closely modeled on Stalin's earlier plans, and Peking placed great stress upon the need for China to utilize "advanced Soviet experience." Although the Russians provided only limited financial aid to China, they sent thousands of technicians, blueprints, and machines, which formed the essential core of the Chinese industrialization program in its early stages. They also helped Peking, during and after the Korean War, to modernize its army and to build substantial military strength. Internationally, Peking and Moscow closely coordinated their policies toward the non-Communist world, and ideologically China and Russia seemed to view the world through the same lenses.

Under the surface, there were tensions, even in these early days, caused by Stalin's highhanded methods. But the Sino-Soviet alliance remained firm, and its two partners presented a front of "unbreakable friendship" and "monolithic unity" in their dealings with the non-Communist nations.

In the period immediately following Stalin's death, the unity of the alliance appeared, if anything, to be

strengthened, as Peking received increasing deference
from Moscow. Then, in 1956, a subtle change began to
take place in Sino-Soviet relations. When Khrushchev
"de-Stalinized," the Chinese Communists reacted with
a notable lack of enthusiasm. And when, in the wake of
de-Stalinization, crises in Poland and Hungary shook
the entire Communist bloc, Peking intervened and
started to play a new role in bloc affairs. The Chinese
began concerning themselves more than ever before
with bloc-wide problems; apparently lacking confidence
in Khrushchev's ability to manage the situation alone,
they took it upon themselves to define many of the
major issues, and the "correct" ideological line on them,
for the bloc as a whole. Paradoxically, in this period, the
Chinese appeared to play a mediating role between
Moscow and Eastern Europe and were, therefore, the
"moderates," whereas subsequently Moscow has assumed
the "moderate" role, and the Chinese have become the
"extremists."

In late 1957, at the Moscow conference of Communist
states and parties celebrating the fortieth anniversary
of the Bolshevik Revolution, a significant difference first
emerged between the Chinese and the Russians regard-
ing the general international situation and its policy
implications for the bloc. The Chinese, apparently believing that the bloc should capitalize on the Russians'
recent technological advances (Sputnik and ICBM), pro-
claimed that "the East Wind prevails over the West
Wind" and adopted a militant new line toward the
West. The Russians, who had only recently absorbed
the full implications of nuclear weapons, drew much

less far-reaching conclusions from their own scientific achievements.

Sino-Soviet policy differences, and decreasing policy coordination, became more and more evident during 1958–59. Many situations and issues were involved: the bloc's treatment of Tito, the Middle Eastern and Que-moy crises of that period, policies toward India and Indonesia, and—most important—the question of a possible summit conference and *détente* with the United States. As Khrushchev moved closer to the summit, the Chinese Communists seemed to become increasingly apprehensive that any Russian-American settlement would make it more difficult for them to achieve some of China's basic goals, such as the recovery of Taiwan and entry into the nuclear club. Sino-Soviet economic relations also began to decline in this period; the last payment of earlier Soviet loans to China was made in 1957, and no further financial assistance was forthcoming.

Then, in 1960, the Sino-Soviet dispute entered a new stage. An intensive ideological debate developed, ranging over a wide variety of issues. Although the arguments were usually veiled, the dispute came out into the open. In Soviet and Chinese publications, and in a series of Communist-bloc meetings, Peking and Moscow argued bitterly about the "inevitability of war" (especially local wars), the nature of "imperialism," the possibility of "peaceful coexistence," the desirability of promoting "armed struggle" in revolutionary situations or of cooperating with the "national bourgeoisie," and the feasibility of pursuing policies aimed at disarmament and *détente* with the West. The debate over these and other issues reached one climax at the end of 1960, during the Moscow conference of eighty-one Communist parties. The declaration resulting from the conference was extremely ambiguous on many of the points at issue, however, and it clearly did not resolve the existing differences.

During that period, as the ideological dispute developed, inter-Party and interstate relations also began to undergo significant changes. During 1957–58, the Chinese started to turn increasingly away from the Soviet economic model and to experiment with new approaches of their own; many of their experiments, including the communes, obviously did not receive Soviet approval. Contacts of all sorts began to decline. Finally, in 1960, virtually all the Soviet technicians and advisers in China returned home.

The dispute became even more overt in 1961, and it ultimately resulted in an open clash over Albania at the Twenty-second Congress of the Soviet Communist Party. Preceding the Congress, while Soviet-Albanian relations had come close to the breaking point, the Chinese and Albanians had steadily formed closer ties. Then, at the Congress, Khrushchev made an open attack on the Albanians for their opposition to his de-Stalinization and coexistence policies. His aim, clearly, was to bring not only the Albanians but the entire bloc, including China, into line. But instead of submitting, the Chinese hit back. Premier Chou En-lai publicly criticized Khrushchev for his attack and walked out of the Congress, and Peking thereafter proceeded to increase its backing of Albania, which by this time had become, in effect, a Chinese rather than a Soviet satellite.

Underlying all the specific issues in the Sino-Soviet dispute as it has developed, especially since 1960, has been the basic question of authority. The Communist bloc has undergone fundamental changes since the death of Stalin; it is no longer a monolithic structure, dominated completely from one center. With the growth of "polycentrism," it has become a complex international system with the lines of authority much less clear than ever before. There are now at least two major centers of authority: Moscow and Peking. The central question is whether these two can subordinate their differences sufficiently to maintain their alliance, or whether the tensions between them are leading toward some sort of overt split.

Until recently, most informed observers have felt that a split was highly improbable. It was believed that despite the changing nature of Sino-Soviet relations, the cohesive elements in the alliance—the common goals, the ideological ties, the military and economic links, and, perhaps above all, the political price that a split would involve—far outweighed the causes of tension and were clearly strong enough to prevent any open break. Since the Soviet Twenty-second Congress, however, the future of the alliance has seemed more uncertain. While a break still seems improbable, for all the reasons cited, there is now a growing belief that at least a greater possibility of open division exists than at any time since 1949.

The consequences of the Sino-Soviet dispute are likely to be of very great importance to the entire international community, however it develops in the period immediately ahead. It has already demonstrated to the world

that the Communist bloc is an evolving group of nations, much more complex than in the Stalinist period,
and it has become increasingly clear that the West can
no longer deal with it as if it were monolithic in its
unity. For Peking, the dispute already poses serious
problems. In 1961, the Chinese Communists had to turn
outside the bloc to solve their food problem, and if
existing tensions continue or grow worse, they may be
forced to re-evaluate a number of their basic policies
and to determine whether to rely almost solely on their
own resources or to try to develop new contacts and
relationships to offset the effects of the deterioration of
their ties with Moscow. If the dispute were to continue
developing and did actually lead to an open break, the
entire configuration of world power would be altered.
Washington, as well as Peking and Moscow, would con-
front an almost completely new situation.

It is clearly not possible to predict today what foreign-
policy tactics Communist China will be pursuing toward
the non-Communist world ten—or even five—years
from now. During the past thirteen years, its tactics
have shifted dramatically and quickly, on several occa-
sions, from militancy to peaceful coexistence and then
back to militancy again. Such tactical shifts could take
place rapidly again. They will be influenced by a wide
variety of factors, such as Sino-Soviet relations, Peking's
estimates of the world balance of power and of political
and economic trends in other countries, the success or
failure of the United States in maintaining an effective
military deterrent in Asia and in competing against
Chinese Communist political and economic influence,

and Communist China's own domestic successes or failures.

The only thing that seems certain is that Communist China's influence on world affairs is destined to grow, steadily and substantially. If China is able to build industrial and military strength rapidly, or if it acquires an independent nuclear capacity, Peking's leaders will doubtless press harder to achieve some of their basic claims and demands. If, on the other hand, Communist China encounters successive internal failures and growing domestic problems—if, for example, China's population continues to increase rapidly, agriculture continues to lag seriously, and domestic pressures become intolerable—it is very doubtful that these trends will give the rest of the world great cause for rejoicing. Assuming that Communist China's totalitarian apparatus does not disintegrate—and, on the basis of the Chinese Communists' record to date, this is the only prudent assumption that can now be made—the result of growing domestic crises and pressures might simply be an increased tendency on the part of Communist China's leaders to seek solutions for their problems abroad.

There are some observers who believe that China's recent economic failures at home and the problems in the Sino-Soviet alliance have forced the leaders in Peking to exercise greater restraint in the pursuit of their foreign-policy aims during the past two years, despite their militant pronouncements. Possibly, this is true. It could be dangerous to assume, however, that the result of prolonged crises in Communist China's foreign relations or domestic situation—particularly if such crises developed to the point where they appeared to

present a real threat to the survival of the regime—
would necessarily impose new restraints on the Chinese
Communists. The result might well, in fact, be just the
opposite.

Communist China is now, unquestionably, one of the
major forces at work in the dangerous world in which
we live, a force with which the rest of the world, Communist as well as non-Communist, will have to deal for
a very long time to come. In China, one-fifth of the
world's population is engulfed in one of the most tremendous revolutionary upheavals of all time. The
leaders of this revolution have extremely ambitious
aims, and in struggling to achieve them they will encounter extremely serious problems. The regime they
lead is already one of the most disturbing factors on the
world scene, and there is little reason to believe that
it will become less disturbing in the near future. The
question of how to deal with this regime, and with the
revolutionary upheaval it represents, will be one of
the most difficult problems facing the entire international community for a long time to come. It is a problem to which Moscow as well as Washington will be
forced to give increasing attention in the years ahead.

N